# Clever Girl Finance

# Clever Girl Finance

*Learn How Investing Works,*
*Grow Your Money*

**Bola Sokunbi**

WILEY

Published by John Wiley & Sons, Inc., Hoboken, New Jersey.
Published simultaneously in Canada.

For general information on our other products and services or for technical support, please contact our Customer Care Department within the United States at (800) 762-2974, outside the United States at (317) 572-3993, or fax (317) 572-4002.

Wiley publishes in a variety of print and electronic formats and by print-on-demand. Some material included with standard print versions of this book may not be included in e-books or in print-on-demand. If this book refers to media such as a CD or DVD that is not included in the version you purchased, you may download this material at http://booksupport.wiley.com. For more information about Wiley products, visit www.wiley.com.

*Library of Congress Cataloging-in-Publication Data*

Names: Sokunbi, Bola, 1981- author.
Title: Clever girl finance : learn how investing works, grow your money /
   Bola Sokunbi.
Description: Hoboken, New Jersey : John Wiley & Sons, Inc., [2020] |
   Includes index.
Identifiers: LCCN 2020021966 (print) | LCCN 2020021967 (ebook) | ISBN
   9781119696735 (paperback) | ISBN 9781119696759 (adobe pdf) | ISBN
   9781119696742 (epub)
Subjects: LCSH: Women—Finance, Personal. | Investments.
Classification: LCC HG179 .S55236 2020 (print) | LCC HG179 (ebook) | DDC
   332.0240082—dc23
LC record available at https://lccn.loc.gov/2020021966
LC ebook record available at https://lccn.loc.gov/2020021967

Cover Design: Wiley
Cover Image: © Clever Girl Finance Inc.

Printed in the United States of America

SKY10021003_090420

*This book is dedicated to all the clever girls who are prioritizing their financial wellness and are focused on building real wealth.*

# Contents

About the Author   xi

Acknowledgments   xiii

You Are in the Right Place! Get Ready to Become
a Clever Girl Investor!   xv

How to Use This Book   xix

Chapter 1     Adjusting Your Mindset About Investing   1
 Why Investing Matters   7
 Getting Educated About Investing   9
 Women and the Investment Gap: Why It's More Important
 Than Ever for Women in Particular to Invest   11
 My Investing Story: The Complete Game-Changer for My
 Finances   15

Chapter 2     How the Stock Market Works   19
 What Is the Stock Market?   21
 Stock Exchanges in the United States   22
 Indices and the Stock Market   23
 The Economy and the Stock Market   26
 How the Economy Affects Your Portfolio   26
 Clever Girl Investor: Meet Jennifer "Jenny" Coombs   30

Chapter 3     Core Investing Concepts: Inflation, Compounding,
               and the Rule of 72   33
 Inflation   36
 What Causes Inflation?   37
 Inflation in the United States   38
 Compounding   39
 How Compound Interest Works   40
 The Rule of 72   44

Compound Interest, the Rule of 72, and Debt   46
Clever Girl Investor: Meet Cindy E. Zuniga   48

**Chapter 4   Preparing to Invest   51**
Key Factors to Ensure You're Prepared to Invest   54
Setting Your Investment Objectives   58
Understanding Risk   59
Mitigating Risk   60

**Chapter 5   The Different Types of Stock Market
Investments   65**
Investing in Stocks   67
Market Capitalization and Stocks   68
Investing in Bonds   70
What to Know About Bonds   70
Should You Buy Individual Stocks and/or Bonds?   73
Investing in Funds   74
Index Funds to Win   76
The Key Benefits of Index Funds   77
Popular Index Funds   79

**Chapter 6   Researching Your Investments   83**
Things to Look for When Researching Investments   86
Extra Credit: More Investing Terms and Definitions   90
Clever Girl Investor: Meet Adeola Omole   92

**Chapter 7   Where and How to Purchase Your Investments   97**
Brokerage Firms and Robo-Advisors   99
Working with a Financial Advisor   102
Practicing with Simulation Accounts   103
Trading versus Investing   104
Clever Girl Investor: Meet Jully-Alma Taveras   105

**Chapter 8   Investing for Retirement   109**
Types of Retirement Investment Accounts   114
What to Do When You Leave Your Employer   122
Tips to Maximize Your Retirement Investments   123
Are You Saving Enough?   126
Investing During Retirement   128
Clever Girl Investor: Meet Faneisha "Fo" Alexander   129

Chapter 9    Simple Investing Strategies   133
The 3-Fund Portfolio Investing Strategy   136
Alternative Investing Strategies: The 1-Fund, 2-Fund, 4-Fund,
and 5-Fund Portfolios   139
Clever Girl Investor: Meet Jamila Souffrant   143

Chapter 10   Keeping Your Investments on Target   147
How Does Rebalancing Work?   149
When to Rebalance Your Portfolio   150
A Common Rule of Thumb: 100 Minus Your Age   151
How Often Should You Rebalance Your Portfolio?   151
Target-Date Funds, Robo-Advisors, and Portfolio
Rebalancing   152
Letting Go of a Losing Investment   153

Chapter 11   The Deal with Taxes   157
Income Tax and Capital Gains Tax   159
Tax Losses   160
Minimizing Your Tax Obligation   161

Chapter 12   Investing Mistakes and Pitfalls to Avoid   165
Key Investing Mistakes and How to Avoid Them   168
Clever Girl Investor: Meet Regina Byrd   170

In Closing   175
Takeaways to Remember   177

Index   181

# About the Author

Bola Sokunbi is a Certified Financial Education Instructor (CFEI), investor, finance expert, speaker, podcaster, influencer, and the founder and CEO of Clever Girl Finance, a personal finance platform that empowers women to achieve real wealth and live life on their own terms.

She started Clever Girl Finance in 2015 to provide women with the tools and resources she wished she had when she began her financial journey.

Bola is also the author of the book *Clever Girl Finance: Ditch Debt, Save Money and Build Real Wealth*.

Today, she lives with her husband and twins in New Jersey.

# Acknowledgments

To my dear husband and children, for cheering me on while I spent late nights and early mornings working on this book.

To my parents, Tunji and Emily, for all your support and advice on this journey.

To team CGF, Esther Bangura, Yazmir Torres, Anita Wikina, and Stacy Jeffries. Thank you for being part of the village helping to make Clever Girl Finance a success.

To the women who have contributed to this book—Jenny Coombs, Adeola Omole, Faneisha "Fo" Alexander, Jamila Souffrant, Jully Alma Taveras, Cindy Zuniga, Regina Byrd, Yezmin Thomas, Kalyn Chandler, Nicole Hatcher, and Sheryl Hickerson—thank you for empowering other women to achieve success by using your voices and allowing me to share your stories.

An extra-special thank you to Adeola Omole for supporting my research into the Canadian resources mentioned in this book and to Kate Braun for working with me through my edits.

To the incredible team at Wiley for working tirelessly to make this book a success, and to all the clever girls ready to build real, long-term wealth, who inspired me to write my second book.

Thank you so much.

Bola

# You Are in the Right Place! Get Ready to Become a Clever Girl Investor!

You probably picked up this book because you've heard about investing time and time again. It's what the wealthy do to get and stay wealthy. It's that thing that you've heard you should be doing—*basically, if you want to build long-term wealth, you need to invest.*

It's the advice you hear consistently in the media, in books, and from various other sources. But perhaps the more you hear people talk about investing, the more overwhelmed you get.

It might be confusing to you. You might be wondering how others have done it. You may have even thought at one point that maybe it's just not for you because, well, you just don't understand how it works and the only thing you hear friends say about investing is how much money they've lost.

But you are still curious. Somewhere in the back of your mind, you've imagined what it would be like to become a successful investor gazing proudly over your portfolio and the wealth you've built.

You've imagined how you can leverage that wealth to pursue your dreams, live life on your own terms, pass down generational wealth, give back to your community, help others, and have financial peace of mind. All while your investments are continuously working for you.

You may have also picked up this book because you've read my first book, *Clever Girl Finance: Ditch debt, save money and build real wealth*, and are ready to level up your investing game now that you've built a solid foundation to achieve financial success.

Either way, you, clever girl, have made an excellent decision to put your money to work for you . . . and you are in the right place.

Investing *is* how the wealthy build and maintain real wealth. It essentially puts your money to work for you, lets you reap the returns of a flourishing economy, and in turn helps you accomplish your financial goals. However, in order to become that successful investor, you need to first understand how investing works so you can make informed decisions. You also need to have a solid plan along with clear objectives and strategies so you can achieve that success.

Keep in mind that when I say *you need to understand investing,* I'm not saying you need to become the next hotshot hedge fund manager (although we absolutely need more female representation in this field). Instead, by *you need to understand investing* I mean looking at the perspective of what *you* need to know personally in order to accomplish your long-term financial goals in the simplest way possible.

It's like the difference between becoming an automotive engineer building the next generation of driverless cars versus knowing how to drive a car safely, following the signs to get to your destination intact, enjoying the ride and scenic views, and arriving happy and excited to have reached your destination. So, with that being said, in this book I'll be breaking down exactly how investing works and more importantly how you can make it work for *you*.

You'll learn how to adjust your mindset about investing (yup, we'll be ditching those fears and any negative thoughts you may have picked up), why investing matters (especially for us as women), how the stock market works, and the core investing concepts you need to know, as well as how changes in the economy can impact your investments (including how to leverage events like economic recessions to your benefit!).

In addition, you'll learn about preparing yourself to invest, different types of stock market investments (how they work, how to research them, and how to buy them), all about retirement and non-retirement investing and how to work both at the same time, managing and minimizing risk, investing pitfalls to avoid, planning for taxes, and ensuring your plans stay on target.

Finally, we'll work through how you can create an overall approach that works for *your life*, leveraging the right tools and resources. *Your life* being the key here because the goals and objectives you have for your life are unique to you.

As with my first book, you and I won't be taking this journey alone. Throughout these pages, you'll read and learn from the personal stories of other women (my "clever" girlfriends) who overcame their investing fears, recovered from mistakes, and have achieved incredible success with investing.

You'll also get tips and key insights from investing experts I've met and worked with along the way on how you should be approaching your investments as you embark on this wealth-building journey.

# How to Use This Book

I've written this book to help you become a more confident and successful investor. With that said, here are some tips to help you get the most out of this book:

- I encourage you to pace yourself as you go through this book and leverage it as a guide as you start working on investing.
- At the end of each section, you'll find practical action steps to help you make progress and take the steps toward becoming a successful investor. Make time to work through these action steps as you develop your investing plans and establish your portfolio.
- You can choose to read through this book in one go and then come back to review your action steps, or you can do the action steps as you get through each section. Pick the approach that works best for you, but set the intention that you *will* take the necessary action. Your future self will thank you. *(Insert hugs and high-fives from you to you here!)*

For additional resources like our articles, podcast episodes, educational videos, and free personal finance courses, visit clevergirlfinance.com and be sure to participate in our amazing community.

I'm so excited for you to get started!

Are you ready?

Let's do this!

CHAPTER 1

# Adjusting Your Mindset About Investing

# Adjust your mindset; empower yourself to succeed.

The way you think about investing makes all the difference in whether or not you'll actually become a successful investor. That's why I believe it's so important first to adjust your mindset around investing, especially if you've had any negative thoughts or feelings toward it in the past. The last thing you want is for your own thoughts to be the roadblock in the way of the success you can achieve.

Some common things many of us tell ourselves about why we can't or shouldn't invest include:

*Investing is too hard. I could never learn how to do it.*

*Investing is only for rich people. They have extra money to burn.*

*Investing is the same as gambling. I might as well hit the slots in Vegas.*

*Investing is scary and I work too hard for my money to take those types of risks.*

Do any of the above statements sound familiar? In the past when you've thought about investing, you may have felt anxious, overwhelmed, confused, or stressed-out. Well, girlfriend, let's change that.

Here's the truth:

- *Yes,* investing can be hard to do, but it doesn't *have* to be if you have the right plan and strategy in place specific to your unique needs.
- *Yes,* rich people invest their money. For the most part, this is how they've built their wealth. But so can you! With commitment, discipline, and knowledge you can even join the ranks of the wealthy yourself.
- *Yes,* many consider investing a gamble. And it certainly can be if you don't know what you're doing! But since you're reading this book, you're definitely not about that "gambling away your hard-earned money" life. And yes, you work really hard for your money, spending hours commuting to work, working on tasks and projects,

attending meetings, dealing with bosses and colleagues. It makes sense that you'd be apprehensive about investing after all the work you've had to put in to earn it. But in reality, investing is a way to make the most of that money and enable yourself to work less.

So, let's take the first step together right here. Decide to drop all the assumptions you have about why you can't invest and why you can't be good at it if you do.

Instead, look at it this way: investing is like learning a different language. Stick with me for a moment while I illustrate. Imagine you move to a country where you don't speak the language, but you need to get directions to a particular destination. You walk up to someone to ask for help and get a flurry of information in this language that you don't understand. They're pointing their finger in various directions, but you have no idea where they are telling you to go. You'd be pretty frustrated, right?

But then imagine that you decide to take matters into your own hands and fully experience all this new country has to offer—including the language. Not only would it make your life so much easier, but you'd also enjoy the experience of living in this new country so much more because you'd actually understand what was going on around you.

So, you buy a language dictionary and start taking language classes. After a few weeks or months, you'd be able to piece together phrases, then full sentences, and before you know it you'd be speaking the language fluently without giving it a second thought.

Investing is very similar. It takes time to learn, but with consistency and discipline you can get the hang of it and really grow your money. The key here is educating yourself, getting informed, and very importantly, conditioning your mindset for success.

Whatever doubts you've had about investing in the past, let them go. You are taking a new path here—one that is going to equip you with everything you need to be a successful investor.

## Take Action

1. In a notebook or spreadsheet, create two columns. In the first, write down every fear or negative thought you have when it comes to investing. It can be based on your past experiences with investing if you've had any, or simply based on what you've heard from others or seen in the media. For example, one could be "I'm worried I'll lose my money in a recession."

2. In the second column, write down all the things you wish you knew or would like to learn about investing that would help you counter each of the fears you've written down. Using our same example of a recession, the thing to learn could be "How to respond to a recession while investing."

3. Keep this list handy as you go through this book. Check off the items you learn as you go along and cross out the fears next to them in the process. The more you know, the more confident you'll be as an investor and the fewer fears you'll have.

*Clever girls know . . . Investing is an essential part of being able to achieve the big financial goals you have for your life.*

## WHY INVESTING MATTERS

In today's world, there are only two ways to make money.

The first way is the traditional one: working. We all know about this one. You receive income for performing a service and essentially trading your time for money. This method encompasses things like working for an employer part-time or full-time, working for yourself actively in your business creating a product or service, working with clients on a freelance basis—effectively, anything that requires you to wake up in the morning and get to work.

The second way is by putting your *money* to work for *you*, where your active participation is not constantly required. For instance, this could mean investing passively in real estate and charging rents that not only cover your expenses but net you a profit. It could mean investing in a business venture that's run and managed by others. Or it could mean investing to earn portfolio income via the stock market (what this book is about!), meaning the money you earn from gains and dividends of stocks in your portfolio. (If you're not 100% sure what a dividend or portfolio is yet, we'll get there.)

You might be saying to yourself, "Well, I save my money in the bank." However, while savings accounts can be excellent for the short term (e.g. saving for emergencies, saving to buy a home, saving for a wedding, etc.), the truth is that they are less successful for the long term. Interest rates are typically so low that you'll never be able to earn more than what you save—especially when you consider inflation, which will eat away at the actual value and purchasing power of your savings.

Plus, keep in mind that in order to have the money to save in the first place, you need to exchange many hours of your time for money *and* spend less than you earn. After all that work it would be a shame for your money to lose value or remain stagnant.

To really help you home into what I'm saying, I'll repeat a key point: *When you save your money in a bank account, you'll never be able to earn much more than the amount you save.*

Back to stocks: How exactly do you earn money in the stock market? Well, as an investor, you can earn money from:

- **Appreciation.** This is what happens when the invested assets you own increase in value.

- **Interest payments.** This is money you earn from buying investments like bonds, where you lend money to a corporation or to the government and they guarantee interest in return.

- **Dividends.** These are payments that companies issue to their stockholders based on profits earned.

Because there are multiple ways to earn money by investing in the stock market, there is the opportunity for you to diversify your investments and earnings. As you continue doing this over time, your money earns money, and then *that* money earns money (this is called *compounding*), so we are talking about potential exponential growth here. This can all multiply far beyond what you are able to earn by exchanging your time for money and putting it in a savings account. Not to worry, we'll be getting into more details on how all of this works later.

So why does investing matter?

It matters because regardless of how you do it, it's the one way in which you can put your money to work for you so you can increase your income without increasing your workload and build the life you truly desire. If you've ever thought about retiring early into the lap of luxury, traveling the world with loved ones, owning a beautiful home or even multiple homes, having the freedom to work on your passions, being able to be generous with loved ones and charities, or any other dream that money can empower you to achieve, then investing is how you get there. If you're wondering how the truly rich get and stay rich, investing is the answer. That's right—no magic tricks!

That's why investing matters.

## GETTING EDUCATED ABOUT INVESTING

By now you get why investing matters. You need to invest to grow your money, point taken. But perhaps you have wondered why you need to know the details of how it all works. After all, these days you can simply input your goals into your favorite robo-advisor tool and it will create a master plan for you. Or better still, you can hire a financial advisor to figure it all out for you. Isn't that what you pay them for? In theory, this sounds great, but realistically not so much.

Getting educated about how investing works is key to being able to make informed investing decisions. And when you're able to make informed investing decisions, you become a better, more confident, and more successful investor.

Don't get me wrong, I'm not saying that you need to become the Queen Bee of Wall Street or take on a side gig as an investment banker in order to invest successfully. What I'm saying is that it's important for you to know what things mean and how things work so that when you put your money in the stock market, you have a good sense of what's happening and how to plan accordingly in line with your financial goals.

Look at it this way: when you purchase a car, you don't really need to know the details of what parts make up the engine, the mechanics of how the seat is designed to recline and move forward, or the science behind how the air-conditioning turns hot air from the outside into cold air on the inside based on the temperature you've set. (If you have an interest in learning how all of that works, that's great, and hey, why not? I'm just saying you can still drive the car either way.)

But what you definitely need to know, at a minimum, is how to turn the car on, how to put gas in it, how to adjust your seat and mirrors, how to drive it (and parallel-park it), and what the traffic rules are depending on where you live. You don't have to know it all; you just have to know enough to get you successfully to your destination. The bottom line is that with most things you do in life, you are going to need to have a bit of knowledge in your back pocket (or Chanel handbag—book #1 readers, you know the backstory!) to make smart decisions.

Before you can automate your investing with your robo-advisor tool, you'll need to input key information so its complex algorithms can come up with an investing strategy for you. But more importantly, you'll also need to understand the strategy it presents to a point where you have a degree of comfort and confidence about how it's going to invest your money and what could potentially happen to it.

The same applies to working with a financial advisor. Before you have your financial advisor go off and create a plan for you, you'll need to have a conversation or a series of conversations with them. And you want your side of those conversations to clearly convey your goals and objectives. You also want to be able to comprehend your advisor's side of the conversation when they start suggesting various investment strategies and approaches to you.

Furthermore, being well-informed will help you avoid being taken advantage of if you do decide to outsource your money management. Perhaps an advisor recommends a subpar investment or charges too high a fee. If you're not educated about investing, you'll be less equipped to notice when something is amiss.

So, like I said earlier, knowing how investing works will help you make informed and confident decisions as an investor and will help you gain peace of mind about your money. Because at the end of the day, as easy and as simple as it might sound to hand everything investing-related off to an automated program or advisor or even avoid it altogether, you don't want to make guesses or blindly trust someone else with your hard-earned money.

## WOMEN AND THE INVESTMENT GAP: WHY IT'S MORE IMPORTANT THAN EVER FOR WOMEN IN PARTICULAR TO INVEST

The statistics on women and investing are pretty depressing. First, there's the gender wage gap that we all talk about, which highlights the inequality issue of women earning 20% less on average than men. And when broken down by demographics, the stats are even more jarring. For every dollar earned by our white male counterparts, Asian women earn 87 cents, white women earn 82 cents, black women earn 65 cents, and Latina women earn 58 cents.

Keep in mind that this wage gap holds true despite our doing the same job functions and having similar work experience and educational backgrounds. Across demographics, the average woman is expected to earn $430,480 less than the average white man over their lifetime.[1] This is not okay.

On top of this, fewer women are investing their money. So, not only are we earning less; we are also not investing enough of the income we are getting. This means that in addition to the wage gap between women and men, there is also an investment gap, which has an even more severe impact on our overall life-time earnings. Especially when it comes to our long-term finan-cial goals, we are not putting enough of our money to work for us.

Why is this the case? It definitely isn't because we aren't smart or good with money, because we darn well are. According to a study by Sofi,[2] women invest more than men do in educa-tion to develop their careers, earning two-thirds of all graduate degrees and half of all master's and doctorate degrees. We are

[1]https://en.wikipedia.org/wiki/Gender_pay_gap_in_the_United_States#By_race.

on top of understanding our debt and how to repay it, paying off our student loans 10% faster than men. Fidelity Investments also shared a study[3] showing that women consistently save a higher percentage of their paycheck than men do.

However, when it comes to investing, women make consistent contributions 48% less than men[4] and are typically much more conservative investors when they do invest. Almost 70% of the money women have is in cash.[5]

Some contributing factors could be the fact women don't have all the support and education they need based on the state of today's financial industry, which is heavily male-dominated. In fact, only 17%[6] of all financial planners are female, which implies that most financial planners may not truly understand the financial planning needs women have.

Surveys[7] show that many women believe their gender is a key factor in how they are treated when seeking financial advice. Many women have complained they they've felt talked down to, stereotyped for their age and gender, or been made to feel like they didn't know what they needed. I've heard stories of this firsthand from women in the Clever Girl Finance community and I can personally attest to this treatment myself.

I vividly remember walking into a financial planning meeting as a young 20-something who needed help understanding investing, only to have the financial planner ask me if I was married and, if I wasn't, where I had gotten my money from. This

[2]https://www.sofi.com/blog/women-investing-gender-wealth-gap-nobody-talks/.
[3]https://www.fidelity.com/about-fidelity/individual-investing/better-investor-men-or-women.
[4]https://www.sofi.com/blog/women-investing-gender-wealth-gap-nobody-talks/.
[5]https://www.businesswire.com/news/home/20150305005794/en/BlackRock-Global-Investor-Pulse-Survey-American-Women.
[6]https://www.investmentnews.com/article/20180808/BLOG09/180809930/the-rise-of-the-female-financial-adviser.
[7]http://image-src.bcg.com/Images/BCG_Women_Want_More_in_Financial_Services_Oct_2009_tcm9-125088.pdf.

line of questioning came after I had excitedly shared my objectives and goals for the money I had been able to save.

Not only did I feel patronized, I was demotivated, and I actually left the financial planner's office completely pissed off and without investing any of my money. It sat in my savings account for a good while before I decided to teach myself how to invest and started investing my money on my own.

All of that being said and despite the fact that there are not enough services and resources to support women with investing, we are more than capable of taking things into our own hands. We can change the statistics and narratives about women and investing for the better, not just for ourselves but for our children, too.

As a woman, it's important to understand that taking advantage of the time you have right now to invest and put your money to work for you is key to building long-term wealth and achieving your financial goals, including living out a retirement that you'll enjoy.

Yes, saving cash in the bank is great for emergencies, upcoming planned expenses, and short-term goals. But when it comes to beating inflation and earning enough returns to grow your money, you are going to need to invest. Keep in mind that since we live longer on average than men, we will most likely need more money to support our future selves when we get older. And whether or not we live longer than our male counterparts, many women are choosing to remain single or are single as a result of a relationship that did not work out, divorce, or the loss of a spouse. This in turn means many of us are navigating our finances as single mothers and sole household earners, making it more important than ever for us to be in charge of our finances.

Investing strategically for growth and being less conservative if you have a long timeline can also have a huge impact on your ability to build wealth. Don't get me wrong, investing conservatively is absolutely not a bad thing, neither is having a mix of risk levels in your investment portfolio. However, there is definitely opportunity to build *more* wealth by being strategically more aggressive, especially when you have time on your side and your goals are long-term. It may feel riskier, and it's true that the market could take a downturn, but having a long-term horizon helps to mitigate the risk because you're investing with time for recovery and growth.

Over time, investing can help you overcome the impact of the wage gap, especially when done consistently. The effect of compounding on your investment returns and earned dividends can greatly amplify the growth of your portfolio. Once you get started with investing, things tend to snowball (in a good way). But sometimes getting started is the hardest part.

As I found out by teaching myself to invest and building a portfolio and assets I'm extremely proud of, it takes purpose, intention, education, action, and consistent assessment to do it. But like I said, we are more than capable. With the right resources and education, women are actually better investors (it's a fact!). We approach investing with a long-term mindset focusing on our financial independence, security, and quality of life. We spend a good amount of time researching our investments, which helps us minimize irrational and impulsive decisions, which in turn allows us to make fewer emotionally driven investments. We invest to win for ourselves, not to compete or show off. Plus, we seek help when we need it.[8]

Even despite the odds stacked against us, women have demonstrated that when given the opportunity, we are this good with money. Don't you feel empowered to put those smarts into play for yourself? Regardless of any mistakes you've made with your finances in the past, right now is a great time to grow your knowledge, build up financial confidence, take the actions to get your finances in order, and leverage the power of investing to build long-term wealth for you and your family.

---

[8]https://seekingalpha.com/article/2071583-men-vs-women-investment-decisions.

The best part of having this book to guide you is that you won't be doing this alone.

## MY INVESTING STORY: THE COMPLETE GAME-CHANGER FOR MY FINANCES

When I started earning my first real salary right out of college, my investment strategy was nonexistent. In fact, investing was the furthest thing from my mind. I had no idea what investing in the stock market was all about or where to even start. As a matter of fact, browsing through my new-hire documentation and seeing the words *401(k)* and *employer-sponsored retirement plan* left me thinking, "Huh?"

I'd never heard of those things before, plus retirement was the last thing on my mind. I was a fresh-faced 24-year-old college grad who was not thinking about anything related to retiring. And if I'm being really honest, I actually initially dismissed the idea of signing up for a 401(k) almost immediately after reading about it, because retirement as it was defined in the guide (age 65) was a whole other lifetime away for me. By then I could be anywhere (living it up in Monaco, Paris, or Miami) and anyone (Beyonce, Oprah). Ah, to be young and naïve.

To give you some more insight as to where my head was, I'll add some color around my thought process during this time. It took me five years to complete my four-year college degree. I was extremely fortunate that along with a partial scholarship to support my tuition costs, my mother paid for my college education. But despite this, there were times that even with my mother's support and my partial scholarship, I had to go to school part-time because my mom didn't have enough money for my tuition and I couldn't qualify for student loans as an international student (which in retrospect was a blessing in disguise). Given the extended time it took me to get through college, by the time I got to graduation, I was ready to make some real money and make it fast.

I wanted to make my parents proud and show my mom that her investment in my college education and the opportunity she provided to me was worth it. And so, once I got my first full-time job, I wanted all my money deposited in my checking account where I could see it, not sent to a random scheme called a 401(k), with words like *fees, expenses, risk, not guaranteed*, and *assumed liability* being used in the description—a scheme that also, in my mind, had no immediate impact on my current day-to-day life. I was like, "Thanks, sounds great, but no thank you very much!"

But then, on the second day of my job's orientation, just as I was getting ready to tune out during the overview of my employer-sponsored retirement plans and their 401(k), I heard the words *free money* and I immediately perked up. I mean, *free* and *money* mentioned in the same sentence? And said by the very important lady from HR, no less? Sign me up! Those two simple words were a complete game-changer for me.

I learned my employer was offering a free contribution match of 100% up to 6% of my own contributions. I might not have known or even cared about the 401(k) at the time, but I sure knew a good deal when I saw one, and so I signed up for my company's 401(k) and made sure I contributed just enough to get the full match they were offering. It took a few months to be fully enrolled, but as soon as I saw how quickly the money was accumulating from my consistent payroll deductions each and every paycheck I got interested in contributing more than was required to get the match. I was also interested in learning more about how investing worked. I started reading books and learned what mutual funds, expense ratios, diversification, and asset allocation were. I even opened my own non-retirement brokerage account and created watchlists for individual stocks that I liked.

Of course, while I was doing all of this, I made mistakes. Tons of them, especially in my non-retirement account. I bought stocks because they were hot. I panicked when the market fell and sold too quickly, losing money as a result. I happily cashed out of stocks that had made returns, only to be deflated when I saw the taxes I had to pay (which I had no idea about) at the end of the year.

However, through trial and expensive errors, I learned how investing worked, established my comfort level with risk, and eventually was able to create clear objectives for myself as a result.

Not too long after, I discovered index funds (which we'll get into in a lot more detail in this book) and how to create an investment strategy using these funds. While I was employed at that first job, my money was invested in the limited mutual fund offerings they had. I built my contributions up to where I was not only getting the full match but also maxing out my allowable contributions. Once I left, four years later, I had well over $70,000 in that 401(k) from my contributions, my employer's match, and the gains I had earned from my investments in the stock market. I couldn't believe it! I then rolled my retirement money over into a traditional IRA and invested my money in my choice of index funds. As soon I was eligible to invest in my new employer's plan, I did that as well. This time, not only was I getting my employer's full match, but I decided to fully max out my contributions right away.

In five short years, the retirement plan I had with my new employer grew to over $100,000. Again, I was shocked, because I had really just set it and forgotten all about it. Since I began contributing to the plan almost right away, I didn't give myself a chance to get used to seeing that money included as part of my paycheck, so I didn't miss it. Instead, I was focused on my investments in my non-retirement accounts, my savings, real estate, and my side hustles. Yes, there were dips and spikes in the stock market, but despite that, there was growth over time (thank you, dividends and compounding!).

Combining my retirement plan investments with my non-retirement investment accounts and my other savings, I had built up a pretty sweet portfolio of assets. And to think that this would have been a different story if I had listened to that little voice in my younger self's head that thought investing was a random scheme and instead had been like *"Nah,* I'll pass," when it came time to sign up for that very first 401(k). That small action became the catalyst for the investments I made in my employers' plans, my interest in learning about how investing worked, my actions of setting up my non-retirement accounts and growing my portfolio, and now this very book you have in your hands on the topic of investing.

Today, I continue my investing journey alongside my husband. I'm also now investing for my children's futures and teaching them how to invest in order to give them an even better head start than I had. My goal is to pass down not just generational wealth, but knowledge and good financial values as well.

Looking back, my investing story is an example of the saying "little drops of water make a mighty ocean" and a reminder that all you have to do is simply get started. It's easy to overthink yourself into a standstill, fear the unknown, and let inertia stop you from doing anything at all. But, when you set the intent to succeed and start taking action, no matter how small at first, it's just a matter of time before you start to reap the rewards.

CHAPTER **2**

# How the Stock Market Works

# Knowing how things work changes the game.

n order to really understand investing and how it works, a great place to start is with the stock market itself. The stock market is probably the first thing that comes to mind when you think about investing. And you can't talk about investing in stocks without mentioning the stock market itself.

You've probably heard references in the media or in conversation to things like stock exchanges, indices, bull and bear markets, and more. Maybe these terms sound unfamiliar to you, or you have a vague understanding of what the stock market is. Either way, that's fine. In this chapter, I'll be breaking down just what the stock market is, how it works, and what you need to know about it.

## WHAT IS THE STOCK MARKET?

The stock market is basically where buyers and sellers trade assets like stocks (also known as shares or equities) and bonds.

**A stock** represents an ownership share in a company. They are sold by corporations who want to raise capital to fund the growth of their business. Stocks rise and fall in value based on what buyers are willing to pay for them and what sellers are willing to take for them. People make money from investing in stocks either from buying low and selling high, or from compounding growth over time based on valuation and dividends earned.

**A bond** on the other hand is basically a loan that you, the investor or bond holder, can make to a borrower (e.g. the government or a corporation) that is trying to raise large amounts of money. This loan is tied to a maturity date and a specified interest rate at the time you make this loan. As a bond investor, you'd earn money from interest paid over time based on the bond agreement in place. At the maturity date, you receive your initial investment back as well. It's commonly referred to as an "I owe you" investment.

There are other more complex asset types like futures, options, and swaps (also known as derivatives) that are typically traded in the stock market by financial institutions, financial professionals, and advanced traders.

Did I hear you say *"deriva-what?"* I thought so! I only mention them as an FYI because it's good to have an idea of what else can be traded in the stock market. However, from the perspective of being a clever girl investor building long-term wealth and as it relates to this book, you don't need to worry about them. It's just good to know they exist. We'll be delving into stocks and bonds in more detail later on.

Now that you know what the stock market is, let's talk about stock exchanges. While terms like *stock market* and *stock exchange* are commonly used as one and the same thing, they are slightly different. The stock market, as described earlier, is more of a general, overarching term referring to the entire buying and selling market of stocks, bonds, and other asset types. Stock exchanges are more specifically the actual infrastructure set up to support these trades when they happen. Stocks, bonds, and other asset types are listed for sale and purchase on the stock exchange. Multiple different stock exchanges exist, domestically and internationally.

## STOCK EXCHANGES IN THE UNITED STATES

In the United States, there are three main stock exchanges that you've probably heard about in the media or in passing conversation:

1. The New York Stock Exchange, commonly referred to as the NYSE (and also the world's largest stock exchange[1])
2. The National Association of Securities Dealers Automated Quotation System, commonly referred to as the NASDAQ
3. The NYSE American, formerly known as the American Stock Exchange or AMEX

---

[1]https://en.wikipedia.org/wiki/New_York_Stock_Exchange.

All three exchanges are based in New York City, which today is the major financial hub in the United States and largest financial hub in the world. While there are other smaller stock exchanges, these three are where most buying and selling of stocks and other securities happens.

The U.S. exchanges have a wealth of history behind them and some date back many decades (e.g. the NASDAQ) and even a few centuries (e.g. the NYSE). If you are interested, Investopedia.com[2] has a very interesting historical overview of the U.S. stock exchanges.

**In Canada**
The main stock exchange in Canada is the Toronto Stock Exchange, commonly referred to as the TSX and Canada's largest stock exchange. Other smaller exchanges include the TSX Venture Exchange (TSX-V) and the Canadian Securities Exchange (CSE),[3] both of which focus on stock market trading for emerging companies.

**Outside the United States or Canada**
You can find a comprehensive list of global stock exchanges based on the country where you are located on wikipedia.org at https://en.wikipedia.org/wiki/List_of_stock_exchanges.

## INDICES AND THE STOCK MARKET

Now that you have a good sense of what the stock market is and about the stock exchanges where the actual trading happens, let's get into how stock market performance is measured.

Stock indices, also simply referred to as indices (or indexes), are also commonly mentioned when the stock market is discussed. Indices are made up of groups of stocks aggregated according to

---

[2]https://www.investopedia.com/articles/07/stock-exchange-history.asp.
[3]https://en.wikipedia.org/wiki/Category:Stock_exchanges_in_Canada.

different industry sectors, a country's total stock market, or the global stock market. As defined by the Motley Fool:[4]

> A stock index is used to describe the performance of the stock market, or a specific portion of it, and to compare returns of investments.

In simple terms, a stock index is a benchmark or performance measurement for your investments. It's useful when you compare the historical and current performance of the index to the performance of your current investments as a way to gauge how your investments are doing. There are over 5,000 indices that make up the U.S. stock market, but three of the most followed indices are:

1. **The Dow Jones Industrial Average (DJIA).** Commonly referred to as the Dow Jones; measures the stock performance of 30 large corporations from various industries in the United States that are publicly traded on the U.S. stock exchange. Since this index only measures 30 companies, it does not necessarily indicate how the overall stock market is doing.

2. **The Standard & Poor's 500 index.** Commonly referred to as the S&P 500; measures the stocks of approximately 500 large corporation in the United States that have their common stock listed on the NYSE or NASDAQ and make up ~75% of the U.S. stock market.

3. **The NASDAQ Composite.** Commonly referred to as the NASDAQ; measures the stock of over 3,000 corporations primarily in technology, but also in the financial, industrial, insurance, and transportation industries both in the United States and internationally.

For the performance of the overall U.S. stock market, the **Wilshire 5000 index** measures almost all publicly traded

---

[4]https://www.fool.com/knowledge-center/what-is-a-stock-index.aspx.

U.S. corporations and can be used as a representation of how the overall stock market is performing. It's made up of over 6,700 publicly traded companies.

Indices are an important part of the stock market and the economy as a whole, since they measure the performance of the companies in various industry sectors that make up the stock market and contribute heavily to the economy itself. Later we'll

---

**In Canada**

In the Canadian stock market, some of the most-followed indices include:

1. **The S&P/TSX Composite Index**, which measures approximately 70% of total market value of the companies traded on the Toronto Stock Exchange (TSX) with about 250 companies included.
2. **The S&P/TSX 60**, which measures 60 large companies listed on the Toronto Stock Exchange covering 10 industry sectors.
3. **The S&P/TSX Venture Composite Index**, which measures 500 publicly traded companies on the TSX Venture Exchange (TSX-V) that do not meet the criteria to be listed on the larger Toronto Stock Exchange (TSX).

**Outside the United States or Canada**

To find the popular indices for your country, simply do a Google search on "stock indices" for your country's name. There are a number of comprehensive lists of major world indices online, including lists on the following websites: finance.yahoo .com (https://finance.yahoo.com/world-indices), investing. com (https://www.investing.com/indices/major-indices), and wikipedia.org (https://en.wikipedia.org/wiki/List_of_stock_ market_indices).

get into how investing in index funds can be used as a long-term wealth building strategy.

## THE ECONOMY AND THE STOCK MARKET

Now, let's talk about the effect of the economy on the stock market. The performance of the economy has a direct impact on the performance of your investments in the stock market.

Whether the economy is growing or in decline (a period usually referred to as a recession), its state at any given time impacts how much money is available and being spent, and also impacts the demand and supply of goods and services. As a result, the economy influences the performance of the stock market, because the companies (businesses) that make up the stock market are also driven by supply and demand.

The performance of these same companies ties into job creation and employment or the lack thereof and influences how comfortable people are with spending money depending on how the economy is doing. In growing economies there are typically lots of jobs available and people typically spend more money because they feel good that the economy is doing well, whereas in recessions unemployment is higher and people are typically more cautious with the way they spend money due to a higher feeling of uncertainty. Basically, all of these things boil down to what is typically known as economic cycles.

## HOW THE ECONOMY AFFECTS YOUR PORTFOLIO

As you start to think about investing now and into the future, it's important to understand the direct impact the economy and stock market have on your investments. The behavior of the economy can affect your portfolio in several ways, including:

- **Through inflation.** Inflation is essentially the increased costs of goods and services and the decline of the purchasing power that money has. For instance, inflation can cause the same exact product (like bread or milk) to cost more today than it did five years ago. High inflation reduces the purchasing power of the dollar, so $50 now will buy you fewer groceries than it used to. Since high inflation can make it expensive to buy goods and services, it discourages consumers from making as many purchases. This causes companies to have lower sales and in turn less revenue, in which case their stock value could fall.

On the other hand, low inflation means people have more spending power and companies are doing well with sales and revenue, which in turn causes their stock value to rise. This rise and fall of stocks in relation to inflation directly affects your portfolio because if the value of a stock you own falls, your investment is worth less, and if the value of the stock increases, your investment is worth more in turn.

■ **Through changes in interest rates.** Interest rate targets are set by the Federal Reserve. These interest rates help determine what it costs to borrow money from your bank, credit card company, or other type of lender, as well as how much interest you're paid (e.g. in a savings account). Banks and lenders can still set their own specific rates, which is why you will find higher and lower interest rates from different institutions, but usually they will all respond in some way to changes in Federal Reserve targets. Typically, interest rates are raised in strong economies to manage excessiveness and lowered in declining economies to encourage spending.

When interest rates increase or decrease, the value of stock prices can be indirectly affected as well. For example, if interest rates are increased, the interest rate on mortgages for prospective home buyers will be higher. In turn, monthly mortgage payments will also be higher. When people have higher mortgage payments, they also have less discretionary income to spend, which can impact the sales and revenues of businesses that are publicly traded in the stock market. In turn, of course, the value of their stock and your portfolio can decline.

- **During bear markets.** A "bear market" is a term commonly mentioned when the stock market is being discussed. Basically, during bear markets, stock prices are in decline, and this makes investors nervous. (The name literally makes me think of bears hibernating in caves; the economy is just hibernating, too!) A bear market usually goes hand in hand with a flat or declining economy. Often, investors see these declining prices, panic, and sell their stocks, often at a loss, because they're afraid of further declines. Panicking, however, is not a good idea, especially when you have time on your side and can weather the storm. In fact, a bear market could present great opportunities to buy stocks that are undervalued. In other words, it could be described as "the stock market on sale," because when stock prices are lower, you can buy them for cheaper. A bear market is a great time to revisit your financial objectives and make sure they're right for you.

- **During bull markets.** This is another commonly mentioned term. If a bear market is hibernating, a bull market is charging. During bull markets, stock prices rise, investors gain confidence because their investments are making money, and as a result they are motivated to buy, buy, buy. And who doesn't love that?! Bull markets are typically high-growth times.

---

**When does a bull or bear market occur?** Typically, a shift of 20% or more from a recent peak or low can trigger an "official" bear or bull market.[5] So basically, if stocks or indices fall more than 20% over a period of time (two months or more), it's considered a bear market, and if they rise more than 20% over a given period of time, it's considered a bull market.

---

[5]https://www.investopedia.com/ask/answers/bull-bear-market-names/.

- **During market bubbles.** In market bubbles, stocks are typically overvalued, and prices of stocks are much higher than they are worth. The bubble eventually bursts, as all bubbles do, and prices fall. Bubbles usually occur with "hot" investments when everyone is rushing to buy and inflating the actual value of the investment. A good example of this was the real estate bubble that burst, causing the 2008 financial crisis and recession due to overvalued real estate, easy access to financing (even when people could not afford it), and a lot of speculative behavior on the part of investors. Investors who buy "hot" investments at the height of a bubble usually lose the most. Unfortunately, the impact of market bubbles in specific industries can trickle into other industries and markets. For instance, the 2008 recession had a global impact. So, when it comes to investing, relying on hot stocks is not the way to go.

In summary, when it comes to the economy's behavior and how it impacts your investments, the goal (which this book will help you with) is to ensure your overall portfolio is well-diversified and you have clear objectives and a simple yet effective long-term strategy to build wealth regardless of bears, bulls, or bubbles.

## Take Action

Understanding how the stock market works is a key foundation to becoming a successful investor. You don't have to know all the complexities, but understanding the basics will add to your financial confidence. So, do this:

1. Take some time to go over this chapter again if needed.
2. If you'd like to take things a step further, visit the various resources mentioned throughout the chapter for more detailed information on how the stock market works.

## CLEVER GIRL INVESTOR: MEET JENNIFER "JENNY" COOMBS

Jennifer "Jenny" N. Coombs, CRPC®, is an associate professor at the College for Financial Planning. She is the creator, lead author, and lead instructor for the Chartered SRI Counselor™ (CSRIC®) designation education program, which is the first sustainable, responsible impact investing financial designation education program in the United States. She also serves as a subject matter expert on a number of the College's investment courses and serves as the chair of the College's Research Committee. In her spare time, Jenny runs the website Grad Money (gradmoney.org), which she founded to help recent graduates demystify investing in the stock market.

**Q. As someone with a strong investing background and who currently works in the financial planning field, how does a beginner navigate through the sometimes unnecessary complexities of investing?**
A. I think that investing is a lot simpler than one would be led to believe. I once had a mentor equate investing to putting together a puzzle: you don't need to have all the puzzle pieces in place to see what the picture will be, you just need enough so that you can see the trend before anyone else does.

**Q. One of the most common statements made about investing is "I don't know where to invest." What are some key things people should consider when trying to figure out where to invest?**
A. This is often the biggest excuse people give for not getting started, but really, it's quite simple: just *get started*. The first place to invest is in companies that you really like or in companies whose products and services you use all the time. For me personally, I eat at Chipotle Mexican Grill at least once per week, so I made sure to buy shares of Chipotle in my IRA because in the long run all those weekly visits will be paid back.

**Q. Do you have any words of caution for new investors making niche or trendy investments?**
A. Never ever put all your eggs in one basket, and never invest in companies or products that you just don't understand. I've heard

horror stories from people whose parents had 100% of their retirement in Enron and when the company collapsed, they lost everything—don't put all your faith in one company.

**Q. Ahead of making an investment, what is the most important thing every investor should consider?**
A. Before making any investment, be sure that you 100% understand the investment, and if you don't understand, seek a professional (i.e. a financial planner, an advisor, a broker, etc.) who can explain it. So many people jumped into Bitcoin too late and lost money because they saw all the hype but didn't understand cryptocurrencies at all. Stick with what you can understand and don't follow the crowd, because odds are even they don't know what they are getting themselves into.

**Q. Can you share your current personal investment strategy?**
A. For the past five years, I've made a conscious effort to consider sustainability in my consumer decisions. As such, I've made this a mission for my own investments as well as for the financial advisors I educate. By considering environmental, social, and governance (or ESG) factors in investment decisions, we not only ensure that we are investing in a more sustainable and ethical future, but we also can get rid of a lot of unnecessary risk in our portfolios as well. It is a strategy that is being implemented a lot more frequently with younger investors looking to tackle issues like climate change and social justice.

# CHAPTER 3

# Core Investing Concepts: Inflation, Compounding, and the Rule of 72

# Compound interest is magical!

I n this chapter we get into the details of some core investing concepts so you can get a clear view of the big picture of how investing allows your money to grow. Once you understand these concepts, you can leverage them to make your investments really work for you.

A lot of times, when investing is discussed generally, the conversation is typically based on losses or gains. How much an investment grew over what time period or how much it lost. These conversations can make it seem like investing is a game of chance based on a random roll of the dice or on some strange mystical algorithm that no one can figure out except its creator.

If I had a dollar for every time I've heard someone celebrate how much money they've made on an investment over time or complain about how they got burned on an investment gone wrong, I'd be a gazillionaire. I hear these conversations all the time. And when it comes to new investors, the resulting trend I notice is usually one of two things.

The "I made so much money on X investment!" discussions can make a new investor excited to dive into investing. Sometimes too excited. In this scenario, they may throw all caution to the wind and choose investments out of excitement and hype without taking time to properly understand and evaluate them.

On the flipside, the "I lost so much money on X investment!" discussions can be totally off-putting, making a new investor write off investing for the foreseeable future because the discussion just validated any or all of the concerns and fears they had about how investing is dangerous. In turn, the new investor leaves the conversation with an "*Mm-hmm*, I knew it" head nod and frown, and their money remains "safe" and stagnant in their savings account.

However, your goal is to be a strategic and confident investor. Understanding core investing concepts and how they work will help you stay objective and avoid impulsive reactions (like choosing random investments or selling in a panic), even when

35

you hear someone share their stories of good or bad fortune in the stock market.

Two such concepts that I think are really key to understand as you become that confident and strategic investor are *inflation* and *compounding*. Both have been briefly mentioned in this book already, but it's time for a deeper dive.

## INFLATION

You know when you hear your parents or older relatives talk about how things were so much cheaper back then than they are now? You might even have some of those memories yourself. I personally remember saving my little pocket money to buy candy as a small child, and today the same candy from the same brand costs much more. *Ahhh*, the good old days! Even from a year-to-year perspective, some things just seem to get more expensive.

*So, what is inflation?* Inflation, typically measured on an annual basis, is defined as a general increase in the prices for goods and services and the decline in the purchasing power of money over time.

One way in which inflation is measured is through something called the Consumer Price Index (CPI), which is a measure of the average change over time in the prices paid by consumers for a market basket of consumer goods and services.[1] This market basket of goods and services includes things like food, personal items, and transportation. You might hear people talking about how the cost of milk or bread has changed over the years. Items like this are included in the Consumer Price Index, which is then averaged over time as one of the ways to determine the impact of inflation.

For example, according to the U.S. Bureau of Labor Statistics,[2] in 2009 ground beef (a consumer good) cost $3.02 per pound.

---

[1] https://www.bls.gov/cpi/questions-and-answers.htm#Question_1.
[2] https://www.bls.gov/charts/consumer-price-index/consumer-price-index-average-price-data.htm.

However, in 2019 the cost of ground beef was at about $3.99 per pound. This means that between 2009 and 2019, ground beef experienced a 24% price increase and an average inflation rate of 2.4% per year. In other words, the same product ended up costing more due to the rate of inflation over that 10-year time frame. The cost change might seem minor, but over time and across various goods and services, these price increases can have a big impact on your purchasing power.

Now that you understand what inflation is, let's discuss its causes.

## WHAT CAUSES INFLATION?

There are a number of reasons why inflation could happen, including the following three:

1. **Increased demand.** This occurs if the demand of goods and services from consumers causes the prices of said goods and services to go up.
2. **Increased costs.** This occurs if the costs to produce certain goods and services causes the prices of said good and services to go up.
3. **Increased supply of cash.** This is where the increased supply of money in the economy (for instance, if the government decides to print more cash) can reduce the value of money since more of it is available.

Keep in mind that there are other factors that also contribute to inflation, like increased import prices that could cause imported goods and services to cost more, rising wages that could encourage people to spend more and increase demand, natural disasters that could cause temporary scarcity of goods and services and in turn raise prices, and even higher taxes that could cause people to spend less. The combination of these reasons (and others) are potential contributors to inflation occurring.

## INFLATION IN THE UNITED STATES

Currently in the United States, the inflation rate has been at about 2% a year over the last several years. This means that every year the value of the dollar has declined by ~2%. The key words to note here are "every year." To bring it closer to home, if you are just depositing your money into a savings account with an interest rate below 2%, you are actually losing money over time. Wondering how it can be possible to lose money on your savings when you are earning interest? Let me explain further.

According to the FDIC[3] and at the time of writing this book, the national average interest rate on savings accounts currently stands at 0.09% APY. That's 1.91% lower than the rate of inflation. Let's look at a realistic example. Let's say in 2014, you spent $100 on a good or service. Well, five years later in 2019, you'd need to have had $108.65 in order to purchase the same thing. If you spent $1,000, you'd need to have $1,086.48 five years later, and if you spent $10,000, you'd need to have $10,864.76. And that's just in five years! Over time, as the amounts increase, what seems like just a small difference can add up to a big deal.

So, as inflation reduces the value of your money over time, one of your goals as an investor is to leverage investing over the long term to help the value of your money not only keep up with but also surpass the effects of inflation.

Based on historical data, the average stock market return on the S&P 500 since its inception in 1926 (including short-term declines and recessions like the one in 2008) has been around 10%.[4] To break things down a little more, between 2008 and 2018, the average return was 6.88%, even taking into account

---

[3]https://www.fdic.gov/regulations/resources/rates/.
[4]https://www.financialsamurai.com/the-average-stock-market-return-is-slowly-declining/.

the massive losses the stock market took in 2008. However, when you lengthen that time horizon to the last 50 years, from 1968–2018, the stock market had an average return of 10.09%.[5] Adjusted for inflation, this comes out to between 7 and 8%.[6] I'm sure you'll agree with me that over the long term, it makes total sense to focus on beating inflation by as much as possible. I'll take 7 or 8% over 0.09% anytime!

> **Outside the United States**
> To see international inflation rates by country, visit cia.gov and search "Country comparison inflation rate."

Now let's get into the concept of compounding.

## COMPOUNDING

Compounding is my absolute favorite thing when it comes to my finances, because it's essentially what allows my money to turn into more money, and my money's money to turn into even *more* money, and my money's money's money—okay, I'll stop. But you get where I'm going, right? There's a reason why compounding is referred to as "magical," "powerful," and "game-changing" when it comes to wealth building. And it's also why everyone who really understands the *magic* of compounding agrees. Compounding is amazing! Let me break it down.

---

[5]https://www.creditdonkey.com/average-stock-market-return.html.
[6]http://www.simplestockinvesting.com/SP500-historical-real-total-returns.htm.

## HOW COMPOUND INTEREST WORKS

When it comes to investing, compounding helps your investments earn more money as the value of your investment goes up. Compounding can take effect in the following ways:

- **Through interest.** Compounding can amplify any interest earned on your investments based on a rate of return. The rate of return (RoR) is the average profit the investment achieves (or is expected to achieve) over a specified time period and is usually depicted as a percentage. This interest is added to your original investment, which in turn can continue to compound at a larger scale over time.

- **Through dividends.** This is a portion of earnings paid by companies to their shareholders based on stock performance. Your dividends can be reinvested on top of your original investment, which in turn will allow for an increased compounding rate.

- **Through capital gains.** These are any profits you earn when you sell an investment. These earnings can then be used toward another investment to take advantage of the power of compounding.

Let's look at a couple of examples showcasing how compounding works using interest.

---

### Example 1:

Let's say you start investing $5,000 a year (or $416.67 a month) at the age of 25 with a goal to retire ~40 years later once you turn 65. We'll assume an average return of 6% (average meaning inclusive of the stock market's declines and growth). After 40 years and with the power of compounding, your investment would be worth **$820,238.42**. If had you just put your money in a savings account for 40

---

years at today's average bank savings interest rate of 0.09%, you'd only have **$203,551.98**. Maybe instead you decide to save with a high-interest online bank and get 2% interest; then after 40 years, you'd still only have **$302,012.33**.

The table illustrates what would happen if you kept investing $5,000 a year. The first column is the total amount of your contributions over time, the second column is the amount of interest/growth alone you'll have earned since beginning to invest, and the third is the two added together for the total portfolio value you could have by each age.

| Age | Total Contributions | Rate of Return (6%) | Total |
|-----|---------------------|---------------------|-------|
| 25 | $5,000 | $300 | $5,300.00 |
| 26 | $10,000 | $918 | $10,918.00 |
| 27 | $15,000 | $1,873.08 | $16,873.08 |
| 28 | $20,000 | $3,185.46 | $23,185.46 |
| 29 | $25,000 | $4,876.59 | $29,876.59 |
| 30 | $30,000 | $6,969.19 | $36,969.19 |
| 31 | $35,000 | $9,487.34 | $44,487.34 |
| 32 | $40,000 | $12,456.58 | $52,456.58 |
| 33 | $45,000 | $15,903.97 | $60,903.97 |
| 34 | $50,000 | $19,858.21 | $69,858.21 |
| 35 | $55,000 | $24,349.71 | $79,349.71 |
| 36 | $60,000 | $29,410.69 | $89,410.69 |
| 37 | $65,000 | $35,075.33 | $100,075.33 |
| 38 | $70,000 | $41,379.85 | $111,379.85 |
| 39 | $75,000 | $48,362.64 | $123,362.64 |
| 40 | $80,000 | $56,064.40 | $136,064.40 |
| 41 | $85,000 | $64,528.26 | $149,528.26 |
| 42 | $90,000 | $73,799.96 | $163,799.96 |
| 43 | $95,000 | $83,927.96 | $178,927.96 |
| 44 | $100,000 | $94,963.63 | $194,963.63 |

*(Continued)*

| Age | Total Contributions | Rate of Return (6%) | Total |
|---|---|---|---|
| 45 | $105,000 | $106,961.45 | $211,961.45 |
| 46 | $110,000 | $119,979.14 | $229,979.14 |
| 47 | $115,000 | $134,077.89 | $249,077.89 |
| 48 | $120,000 | $149,322.56 | $269,322.56 |
| 49 | $125,000 | $165,781.91 | $290,781.91 |
| 50 | $130,000 | $183,528.83 | $313,528.83 |
| 51 | $135,000 | $202,640.56 | $337,640.56 |
| 52 | $140,000 | $223,198.99 | $363,198.99 |
| 53 | $145,000 | $245,290.93 | $390,290.93 |
| 54 | $150,000 | $269,008.39 | $419,008.39 |
| 55 | $155,000 | $294,448.89 | $449,448.89 |
| 56 | $160,000 | $321,715.82 | $481,715.82 |
| 57 | $165,000 | $350,918.77 | $515,918.77 |
| 58 | $170,000 | $382,173.90 | $552,173.90 |
| 59 | $175,000 | $415,604.33 | $590,604.33 |
| 60 | $180,000 | $451,340.59 | $631,340.59 |
| 61 | $185,000 | $489,521.03 | $674,521.03 |
| 62 | $190,000 | $530,292.29 | $720,292.29 |
| 63 | $195,000 | $573,809.83 | $768,809.83 |
| 64 | $200,000 | $620,238.42 | $820,238.42 |

## Example 2:

Let's say you wait a little longer to invest and you start at age 35 with a goal to retire 30 years later at age 65. You start investing $5,000 a year (or $416.67 a month) and have the same average rate of return of 6%. After 30 years, your investment would be worth **$419,008.39** versus **$151,975.26 (0.09%)** or **$202,842.02 (2%)** if you just put your money in a savings account.

This table illustrates what your annual and total contributions could be as well as what the growth of your money could be over that 30-year time period as a result of compounding.

| Age | Total Contributions | Rate of Return (6%) | Total |
|---|---|---|---|
| 35 | $5,000 | $300 | $5,300.00 |
| 36 | $10,000 | $918 | $10,918.00 |
| 37 | $15,000 | $1,873.08 | $16,873.08 |
| 38 | $20,000 | $3,185.46 | $23,185.46 |
| 39 | $25,000 | $4,876.59 | $29,876.59 |
| 40 | $30,000 | $6,969.19 | $36,969.19 |
| 41 | $35,000 | $9,487.34 | $44,487.34 |
| 42 | $40,000 | $12,456.58 | $52,456.58 |
| 43 | $45,000 | $15,903.97 | $60,903.97 |
| 44 | $50,000 | $19,858.21 | $69,858.21 |
| 45 | $55,000 | $24,349.71 | $79,349.71 |
| 46 | $60,000 | $29,410.69 | $89,410.69 |
| 47 | $65,000 | $35,075.33 | $100,075.33 |
| 48 | $70,000 | $41,379.85 | $111,379.85 |
| 49 | $75,000 | $48,362.64 | $123,362.64 |
| 50 | $80,000 | $56,064.40 | $136,064.40 |
| 51 | $85,000 | $64,528.26 | $149,528.26 |
| 52 | $90,000 | $73,799.96 | $163,799.96 |
| 53 | $95,000 | $83,927.96 | $178,927.96 |
| 54 | $100,000 | $94,963.63 | $194,963.63 |
| 55 | $105,000 | $106,961.45 | $211,961.45 |
| 56 | $110,000 | $119,979.14 | $229,979.14 |
| 57 | $115,000 | $134,077.89 | $249,077.89 |
| 58 | $120,000 | $149,322.56 | $269,322.56 |
| 59 | $125,000 | $165,781.91 | $290,781.91 |
| 60 | $130,000 | $183,528.83 | $313,528.83 |

*(Continued)*

| Age | Total Contributions | Rate of Return (6%) | Total |
|-----|---------------------|---------------------|-------|
| 61 | $135,000 | $202,640.56 | $337,640.56 |
| 62 | $140,000 | $223,198.99 | $363,198.99 |
| 63 | $145,000 | $245,290.93 | $390,290.93 |
| 64 | $150,000 | $269,008.39 | $419,008.39 |

Keep in mind that you'd need to factor in the future rate of inflation for more accurate numbers. However, because the average rate of return of 6% that we use in these examples far exceeds today's average rate of inflation, you'd still end up with a pretty nice sum of money regardless. Also keep in mind that in these two examples, the numbers could be significantly higher if you earn a higher average rate of return on your annual investment.

Based on these examples, it's very clear that the power of compounding is magnified the more you invest, the more interest your money earns, and the more time your money is given to grow. So ideally, you want to begin investing as early as you can. Even if you are in your 40s or 50s or beyond, you can still take advantage of the power of compounding over time. In this case, your goal would be to catch up by increasing your investment amounts, which you can do by finding ways to increase your income. For instance, if you invest $10,000 a year ($833.33 a month) with an average rate of return of 6%, you'd have $232,758.77 after 15 years and $548,642.93 after 25 years.

## THE RULE OF 72

Have you ever wondered what it would take (and how long) for your money to double? I definitely wondered in my early investing days, especially after seeing a ton of "double your money!" ads on the web (scams), on local posters (more scams), and today on various social media platforms (scams on scams on scams). Well scams aside, there is a legit way to *potentially* double your money and also to determine how long it could take. Let me introduce you to the cool rule of 72.

**Q. What is the rule of 72?**
A. The rule of 72 is essentially a rule (or an investing magic trick) that can help you estimate how soon your investment will double based on a fixed annual interest rate (hence my use of the word *potentially*, since we can't predict future interest rates).

To determine this, all you need to do is divide the number 72 by the number of the annual interest rate of your investment (or average annual interest rate). This will give you a rough idea of when your investment will be worth twice as much as it's worth today. This table illustrates examples of various interest rates and timeframes:

| Rate of Return | Approximate Time to Double with the Rule of 72 |
|---|---|
| 2% | 36 years |
| 3% | 24 years |
| 5% | 14.4 years |
| 7% | 10.3 years |
| 9% | 8 years |
| 12% | 6 years |
| 25% | 2.9 years |
| 50% | 1.4 years |
| 72% | 1 year |

Based on this table, if you invest a onetime sum of $5,000 that you don't touch at a fixed annual interest rate of 5%, it would take 14.4 years for your investment to double to $10,000.

**Q. What else can the rule of 72 do?**
A. There are some other ways that the rule of 72 can come in in handy. For instance:

- **It can be used to determine the value of the dollar based on inflation.** On a less happy note, the rule of 72 can be used to calculate how long it will take for your money to lose half its value due to inflation. If we divide 72 by today's average inflation rate in the United States of 2% (so, 72/2), assuming the inflation rate remains consistent, the dollar will lose half its value in about 36 years. If the inflation rate goes up to 3% and remains consistent, the dollar will lose half its value in about 24 years.

- **It can be used to determine interest payments associated to debt.** The rule of 72 can also tell you when the amount you owe in credit card debt will double based on the interest rate you are paying to a creditor. Let's say you have credit card debt at an interest rate of 18%. Dividing 72 by 18 tells us your credit card balance will double in 4 years (This is a basic illustration).

**Q. Why does the rule of 72 matter to you as an investor?**
A. As an investor, the rule of 72 is good to keep in mind because it can help you get a sense of how long it will take for your money to grow (or double) in order for you to meet a financial goal or objective that's tied to a specific timeline. Knowing how long it could take can help you fine-tune your savings and investment strategies in order to achieve your financial goals.

## COMPOUND INTEREST, THE RULE OF 72, AND DEBT

Before we move forward, it's important to understand the implications of compounding and debt. So far, we've talked about how compounding can be an incredible ally when it comes to wealth building. However, when it comes to debt, it can literally be your *worst enemy*. Like, the *worst*. Let's go back to the reference of compound interest being magical, but this time including an additional caution: Compound interest is magical...but only if it's working for you, not against you.

In simple terms, when you have debt, be it a credit card, car note, student loan, mortgage, and so on, the longer you take to pay it off, the more expensive that debt will be. Depending on the interest rates on your debt and how interest is calculated (daily, monthly, annually, etc.), compounding can make your debt balance grow out of control if you don't take action. In fact, you can end up paying more in interest alone than the initial amount of money you borrowed! Using the rule of 72 and dividing 72 by your interest rate can tell you how long it could take for your debt to double, though this only applies if you're making no payments on the debt. Adding in payments just makes the math a little more complex than dividing 72.

Making only the minimum payments is better than nothing, but it can still cause your debt to spiral out of control since interest continues accruing on the remaining amount.

**For example:** Let's say you owe $5,000 in credit card debt at a 20% interest rate and have a monthly minimum payment of $125. During your first month, you'd owe about $83 in interest alone, so only $42 of your $125 payment would actually pay down the principal of your debt. If you continue to make the minimum payments, it would take you 5 years and 7 months to pay off this debt, and you'd pay an extra $3,308 in interest alone on top of paying back the $5,000!

We'll talk more about strategies to pay off debt in the next section of this book but get ready to take off your earrings and roll up your sleeves—because knowing what you know now about compounding, if you have debt (especially high-interest debt), it's time to get ready to give it a serious beat-down.

## Take Action

1. Take some time to run your own scenarios on compounding as it relates to your investments or any debt you might have.

2. Google "Compound interest calculator" or "Debt repayment calculator" and pick the one that is easiest and most visually appealing for you to use. These calculators make it easy to plug in different interest rates, monthly payment amounts, and so forth to get the most accurate numbers for your situation.

3. Running these scenarios is helpful to get your mind churning on key actions you can take over specific time periods. For example, finding ways to increase your income to increase your investment contributions or to accelerate paying down your debt.

## CLEVER GIRL INVESTOR: MEET CINDY E. ZUNIGA

Cindy is a commercial litigation attorney and the founder of Zero-Based Budget Coaching LLC (zero-basedbudget.com), where she provides personal finance coaching services to individuals and couples and speaks to audiences about money. She graduated from law school in June 2015 and landed her dream job at a prestigious law firm in New York City, but she had $215,000 of student loan debt from law school to contend with. She decided to immerse herself in the world of personal finance and focused on creating a concrete plan to pay off her debt. Less than five years later, she did just that, becoming debt-free in December 2019. She leveraged her Instagram account @ zerobasedbudget to document her journey to becoming to debt-free and now uses it to share financial tidbits to help women simplify personal finance concepts. Her mission now is to spread the message of financial literacy to women, particularly to women of color like herself.

**Q. Over the last few years you've been focused on paying off your student loans that totaled $215,000; however, you still managed to invest at the same time. What approach did you take in order to do both of these things strategically?**
A. I did two things. First, I invested in the 401(k) plan offered by my employer. At first, I noticed the difference in my paycheck, but after a month or two I got used to it. It honestly felt like effortless investing. I also opened an account with Betterment, a robo-advisor. I consider myself to be a passive investor and was honestly still very new to investing, so I knew that a robo-advisor would be the best fit for me. I answered a few questions about my goals and risk tolerance and was set up with specific investments. When I opened the account, I set up automatic contributions. Every two weeks I had $40 taken from my checking account and deposited to my investing account. I've gradually increased my contribution amounts since then.

**Q. You are now debt-free. What were some key things you did to pay off your student loan debt?**
A. I was very mindful of the "big three" expenses: rent, food, and transportation. Living in NYC is expensive, but there are ways to keep your costs low. When I graduated from law school, instead of moving into a fancy high-rise apartment in the middle of the city, I stayed in my studio apartment in Harlem. About a year later I moved in with my partner and share the rent costs for our one-bedroom apartment. A decent lunch and a snack in NYC can easily cost $15. I meal-prepped my lunches and snacks for four of the five weekdays, allowing myself to buy lunch on Fridays as a treat. I don't use any food delivery apps because those delivery fees add up fast! Also, because I live in NYC, there is no real need for a car so I not only saved on the cost of a car, but also on insurance, gas, tolls, parking, maintenance, etc.

**Q. Now that your debt is paid off, how will you be accelerating your investing plans and what does your investment approach look like?**
A. I'm not planning on increasing my lifestyle by much, so I plan on putting most of the money that I was using to pay off my debt toward investing. I will likely look into low-cost index funds because, as mentioned, I take a passive approach to investing and want to have a well-diversified investment portfolio.

**Q. As a woman, why is investing so important to you?**

A. My parents immigrated to this country with practically nothing. They weren't able to teach me about investing because they were too busy trying to put food on the table. As the daughter of immigrants, it is my duty to show my parents that all of their sacrifices were well worth it and to help them financially as they get older. I want to build real generational wealth so that my children and my children's children will never lack and will benefit from the seeds that I plant today. I also want to show young women of color that look like me or have life experiences similar to mine that wealth building is possible, but it's crucial to start today.

**Q. What advice would you give your younger self about debt, savings, and investing?**

A. When I was younger, I viewed money as something to spend or save for something that I wanted to purchase in the short term. I never thought about money as something that could make me more money or propel my long-term goals. I would tell my younger self to follow a 10/40/50 rule: give back with 10% of your income, for instance to your favorite charity, a person in need, or as tithes at church; put 40% to your long-term financial goals, whether that's toward investing or paying off debt; and learn how to live on the other half (50%) of your income.

# CHAPTER 4

# Preparing to Invest

*When you are well prepared you are better able to recognize opportunities.*

For some reason, luck is strongly associated with rich people. One of the assumptions often made about everyday people who become independently wealthy is that they've had some miraculous stroke of luck in life that has brought them financial success. While this might be the case for a few outliers (for instance, recipients of inheritances, windfalls, or lottery winnings), the reality is that the "luck" of most everyday wealthy people comes from their setting specific intentions, having the right mindset, and preparing themselves to pursue and achieve the financial success they desire.

Investing in the stock market is a pathway to wealth building, but it doesn't just happen. Becoming a successful investor requires a level of preparation (and patience) to set yourself up for success in the years to come. So, in this chapter we are going to go over the specific things you need to do to ensure that you are well-prepared to invest.

But first, what happens when you *aren't* well-prepared? Here are a few scenarios I've seen play out time and time again. Folks get excited about investing because they read something or heard something somewhere: a hot tip, a hot stock, the next big thing. The stock market looks great. Everything is on the up-and-up and they need to get on the train fast. They put a chunk of money into an investment, with no goals, no objectives, and no idea of their risk tolerance, and then one of a few things happens:

- Something comes up (a car repair, a girl's trip, a job loss) and they need the money right away—this minute, *now*. And so, they sell their investments with minimal or no gains and perhaps they even take on some losses (shout-out to those trading fees).
- After investing, perhaps they see the stock market take a temporary dip a few short weeks or months later. It's all they keep hearing about on the news and in other media, and so panic sets in and they sell their short-lived investments at a major loss.

■ Or maybe they're just having trouble sleeping at night because that's a big chunk of cash they invested in the stock market and right about now it feels like one big massive gamble. Plus they have bills to pay, so just like the previous two scenarios, they sell their short-lived investments with minimal to no gains or with big losses.

If you ask me, these are pretty lousy scenarios. Time has been wasted, hard-earned money has been lost, and they're definitely not getting any of those missed hours of sleep back. Fortunately, if you are reading this book, I know for sure that you are not (or no longer) about that life. You want to know what you're doing before diving in, and rightfully so.

How exactly should you get prepared before you dive into investing? Let's talk.

## KEY FACTORS TO ENSURE YOU'RE PREPARED TO INVEST

There are some key considerations you'll want to keep in mind to make sure that once you start investing, you aren't tapping in and cashing out too quickly because you were ill-prepared. If you don't meet all of the following criteria just yet, don't worry or give up on investing. Just add any areas of improvement to your preparation list so you can set yourself up for success.

**You have an income, preferably a steady income.** It goes without saying that you need money to invest, even if it's just a little bit. When you're starting small, the key to building your investment portfolio is investing consistently over time. Having a steady income will allow you to make these consistent investments. If you're between jobs or trying to find a job and don't have an income coming in, your focus should first be on making enough money to cover your basic living expenses before you start thinking about investing.

**You're able to meet your financial obligations.** While your money is busy working and growing for you in the stock market over the long-term, life goes on in the meantime. That means you still have budgets to create and bills to pay. So, before you start investing, you want to make sure you are able to comfortably meet your financial obligations like covering your day-to-day needs and overall living expenses without having to go into debt in order to survive.

**You have emergency savings in place.** Your emergency fund is there to ensure that you are able to weather life's storms, like a job loss or other unplanned situations. This fund is essentially a backup plan so you don't have to leverage debt or derail your financial goals when these circumstances arise (which they will, because life happens). Establishing your emergency savings should take priority over investing. Ideally, you want to have three to six months of your basic living expenses put aside before you start dedicating money to investing. But before you think this is unattainable, it's important to know that this is referring only to your *basic* living expenses. Essentially, how much do you need at a minimum to pay for your housing, core utilities, food, and transportation? That number sounds more attainable, right? If you have high-interest debt to focus on, then start with $1,000 in emergency savings while the bulk of your money goes to the debt. This can be saved up fairly quickly and can cover the most basic unplanned situations.

**You have paid off your high-interest debt.** Once you have your emergency savings in place, it's time to create a budget and get aggressive with paying down your debt, starting with any high-interest debt you might have. This is important because as we discussed before, interest on debt will compound, and this effect from compounding is essentially like digging a hole with an automatic shovel. Unless you focus on paying off your debt fast (and by that I mean as much as you can possibly afford above the minimum required payment each month), that hole will only keep getting deeper. Your high-interest debt and that damn automatic shovel are the enemy. Attack!

> *An exception: While you are paying down your debt, if your employer offers a retirement plan in which they match your contributions, be sure to contribute enough to get the full match. It's essentially free money and you don't want to leave it on the table. Plus, usually, contributing enough to get the free money comes out to a small percentage that you won't really miss in your paycheck anyway.*

**You have a plan in place for your short-term life changes.** Do you have a life change coming up in the near future that will require financial support, for instance, planning a wedding, preparing for a baby, moving to a new city, or leaving a relationship? If yes, it's important that you plan accordingly by making sure you have money put aside to support your life changes. This isn't money that you should be investing since you know you'll need it in the short term.

**You have the right type of insurance in place.** Having the right insurance coverage can potentially save you a ton of money in the event of an emergency, an unplanned life occurrence, or a medical need. For instance, the right car insurance can pay for the costs of a car accident, like repairs and medical bills. A homeowner's policy can help you rebuild your home after devastating damage from fire or flooding. Health insurance can pay for expensive emergency room bills after an injury or illness. Disability insurance can protect your income in the event you are unable to work for a period of time. No one wishes for bad things to happen, but having the right insurance means you can protect yourself without having to impact your long-term financial plans. On the flipside, not having enough insurance can derail your financial goals and you definitely don't want that.

**You've done your research and have an understanding of what you'll be investing in.** Prior to investing, you should spend some time researching your potential investments with a minimum goal of understanding what they are, what they cost, and how they have performed in the past.

**You understand how much risk you can tolerate.** As an investor, understanding your risk tolerance can make all the difference in how well you sleep at night. Knowing how much risk you can stomach will in turn help you determine how aggressive or conservative of an investor you want to be. Understanding your risk tolerance will also help you eliminate panic when the market is swinging downwards and help you make better buying and selling decisions.

**You have realistic expectations about the long-term performance of the stock market.** The average return of the U.S. stock market based on the S&P 500 since its inception in 1926 has been about 10%. Of course, an average doesn't mean it has been 10% every year. There have been years when the average rate of return has been much higher and the stock market has had double-digit gains above 10%. There have also been years where the stock market has had really major declines and, as a result, double-digit losses. But despite the peaks and valleys, over the long term the average return has stayed consistent. While past performance does not predict the future, it's a pretty good benchmark to use, keeping in mind that you'll want to adjust for that 2% average inflation. This adjustment makes the effective historical rate of return between 7 and 8%. So, when it comes to setting your expectations, especially as a new investor learning the ropes, I recommend being mentally prepared for the losses as well as the gains. When you're crossing through one of those valleys, keep walking toward the peaks.

**You have a plan to diversify your investments.** When it comes to investing in the stock market, it's important that you don't go all-in with one type of stock or one industry. Otherwise, you might find that you've taken on a ton of risk when that stock or industry goes through a rough patch. Having a plan to diversify your portfolio also means that you have a plan to mitigate your risk. It's all about having a good mix of investments.

This way, even if one stock or industry goes down, the others could keep your overall portfolio stable.

*** 

We'll be delving into investment researching, diversification, retirement investing, risk tolerance, and more in upcoming chapters.

## SETTING YOUR INVESTMENT OBJECTIVES

As important as it is to plan to invest for the long term, it's equally important to clearly define your investment objectives in relation to your financial goals. Basically, what are the things that you want your money to be able to accomplish for you in the long term? These goals provide two things: your reasons for investing and how long your investment timeframe is likely to be. Examples of objectives could include things like retiring at a certain age, paying for your child's college education, buying your dream house, creating a family legacy to be passed down through generations, and so forth.

Once you've laid out what your specific investment objectives are, you'll need to:

- Determine how much money you'll need in total for each objective to be met.
- Determine how much you can consistently invest on a recurring basis to help you get closer to achieving your objectives.
- Assign a timeline to your objectives and determine how many years it will take to meet them. (*Tip:* A quick Google search for "investment calculator" will pull up several different calculators to help you determine your numbers.)

As you work on calculating the costs of your objectives, don't worry if the amounts you are able to invest right now aren't enough to meet your objectives within your desired timeline.

Consider that you'll likely have more to invest in the future as you pay off debt, increase your income, and reduce your expenses. Make a plan to adjust your objectives over time as your financial situation changes.

Having clear objectives in place, as well as clear timeframes for them, will help you create a sound investing plan and make the best decisions about how and where you invest your money. For example, if one of your objectives is to retire in a particular year, you can plan to make your retirement investments more conservative as you approach that year. By doing this, you ensure that if there is a market decline around the time when you plan to retire, your investments are protected and you can stay on course with your plan.

As a rule, you don't want to invest any money in the stock market that you have allocated for short-term goals that you want to accomplish within five years or fewer. Why? Well, the stock market is hard to predict, so a lot of volatility can happen over the short term. Investing for the long term (the longer the better) allows you to weather short-term market declines or volatility, because if there is a period of decline, you can patiently wait for the market to recover and grow.

## UNDERSTANDING RISK

When you put your money in the stock market, or in any investment for that matter, you are assuming a certain amount of risk that is unavoidable. Particularly with investing in the stock market, your investments are uninsured and returns are not guaranteed. That sounds scary, but what does it really mean?

Basically, it means that investments can lose their value as a result of company performance, disasters, or other reasons. The stock market can tumble due to economic reasons or political climates. If these scenarios affect stocks you own, then your portfolio could lose value as a result.

However, risk isn't just associated with investing in the stock market. Just about anything you can do with your money carries a degree of risk. For instance, your cash in a savings account is at risk of losing its value over time due to inflation. Buying real estate carries a risk of a property losing value. Opening a business comes with a risk of the business not performing well and having to close its doors. That doesn't mean you should avoid doing these things, either; it just means that when it comes to money, some risk is unavoidable. It's not something to fear, but something you can accept, understand, and work with.

That being said, let's get into some ways in which you can mitigate or hedge against risk.

## MITIGATING RISK

There will always be a level of risk when it comes to investing, which is basically the possibility that you can lose all or some of your money. This same idea applies to life in general. Life is full of risks, some greater than others. You might be employed at a great company, but you run the risk that you could lose your job if the company has a bad year or the finances are mismanaged. You might purchase a top-of-the-line kitchen appliance, but you run the risk that one day it could just stop working for reasons beyond your control like an electrical circuit overload or a defective part. By making a daily commute to work driving in your car, you run the risk that someone could rear-end you even if you are following all the road rules. The list goes on. In life, people either make sure they do everything possible to minimize their risks (e.g. getting a safe car) or they avoid risk altogether (e.g. not going skydiving).

Given the potential for losses, the idea of risk deters many people from investing. Many consider investing a form of gambling—taking a chance on the unknown and hoping for the best. And they are absolutely correct. Investing is basically gambling, *if* you don't know what you are investing in, have no strategy, and aren't clear on your objectives. However, while risk cannot be completely eliminated from any portfolio, there are ways to minimize it. This means taking specific steps to reduce any adverse effects from external factors that are outside of your control but that can impact the value of your portfolio. It is essentially making sure that you don't put all your eggs in one basket.

So, what can you do to minimize risk? Here are three key steps you can take to mitigate your investment risk, in addition to the step you are taking right now, which is reading this book and getting educated on how investing works:

1. **Get clear on your *why* (i.e. your investment objectives).** For each investment you make, it's important that you are clear on why you are investing and when you'll need your money to meet your objectives. Two questions to ask yourself are:

   *Question 1: What are you investing for?* Are you investing for retirement? For your kids' college education? For passive portfolio income? For a home several years from now? Knowing what you'll need the money for can guide you toward the type of investments to put your money into.

   *Question 2: How much time do you have to invest?* If you'll need your money within the next 5 to 10 years, then it makes the most sense to take a conservative approach to investing. That's because you can't time the market and you'll have less time for your investment to recover and rebound from a loss. Say, for instance, if a recession were to happen 3 years into your 5- to 10-year investment timeline, you might be forced to cash out at a loss because you need the money. If, on the other hand, your objective with a particular investment is to save for retirement 30 years from now, then perhaps you could be a bit more aggressive in the short term, then become more conservative as you approach retirement, because you have more time to ride out any short-term losses.

2. **Determine your risk tolerance.** Once your objectives are in place, knowing your risk tolerance is just as critical. Greater returns come with greater risk, but can you stomach possible sharp declines in the value of your investment during a bad market? It's best to determine what kind of investor you are, be it conservative, aggressive, or in between, so you can avoid the stress and headaches from investing outside of your comfort zone. Also, when you understand what you can tolerate as an investor and you have your objectives in place, you are less likely to be swayed by "hot" stocks or recommendations from people suggesting to get in on an investment "*now!*" (no, thank you).

What kind of investor are you? See which of these three types you relate to the most:

*Conservative investor*: If your main focus is to keep your initial investment steady and you're fine with less extreme returns, you are a conservative investor. You are okay with very slight dips in the stock market, especially if you don't need your money in the short term. But if you are only investing for the short term, dips in the stock market could keep you up at night. You don't like surprises and you tend to avoid taking big financial risks. As you approach retirement (when it's less than 10 years away), there's nothing wrong with being a cautious investor. However, if you have a longer time horizon, investing too conservatively can mean sacrificing extra earning potential.

*Assertive investor:* If you have a good sense of risk and understand that the stock market typically always recovers from short-term declines in a matter of time, then you are an in-between or assertive investor. You are comfortable taking more risk in the market and understand market declines could be a great opportunity to get some good investing deals with the proper research. If you still have a while to go (10+ years) before you need your money for an investment objective like retirement, you are okay taking on some additional risk.

*Aggressive investor:* If you are all about maximizing your earnings in the market and you understand that big earning potential comes with big risk, you are an aggressive investor. You are comfortable with large short-term market dips. You typically don't need your money for 20 to 30 years and you are all about growing your portfolio as much as possible. As your time horizon shortens, you may change your investments to be more conservative down the line.

3. **Leverage asset allocation and diversification.** There are two key ways to mitigate or balance out the amount of risk you take on. The first is asset allocation and the second is diversification. These should both be combined to help you create a solid risk mitigation plan. Let's go over what they are:

   *Asset allocation.* This is basically ensuring that you have a mix of different investments in your portfolio (e.g. U.S. stocks and bonds, foreign stocks and bonds, cash, real estate). This way, if one type of investment experiences major losses, the impact to the rest of your portfolio is reduced due to your asset allocation.

   *Diversification.* This, on the other hand, is all about dividing your investments into different categories. For example, by purchasing stocks in different industry sectors like consumer goods, technology, healthcare, energy, telecommunications, and so on, you are creating a well-diversified portfolio. If, for instance, the consumer goods or technology industries experience declines, you still have investments in other industries to balance out your portfolio.

Ultimately, your goal with taking these actions to mitigate your investment risk is to keep your risk in line with your comfort levels while maintaining the value of and growing your investment portfolio. Getting prepared to invest will require some groundwork, but it's well worth the time and effort to make sure that you lay the right foundation for your future success as an investor.

## Take Action

Take some time to ensure you are prepared to invest using the tips in this chapter:

1. Create a debt repayment plan.
2. Lay out your investment objectives: What are you investing for and when do you need the money by?
3. Determine your risk tolerance and the type of investor you are. (Remember, this can and should change over time.)
4. Map out a strategy to mitigate your risk with your current and future investments.

# CHAPTER 5

# The Different Types of Stock Market Investments

*Clever girls know . . . assessing your options is a foundational step for successful investing.*

When it comes to stock market investments, there are a variety of different investment types. In this chapter, we are going to cover the most popular types that commonly make up most portfolios. The reason why it's good to know what types of investments exist (and not just what they are but also how they work) is because this knowledge can help you make the best decisions for your own investment strategies based on your timeline, objectives, and comfort level. So, let's get into the most common investment types and how they work.

## INVESTING IN STOCKS

Stocks, also known as shares, give you an ownership or equity stake in a company. When you buy a company's stock, you essentially become an owner or shareholder. The value of the stock you buy depends on several factors, including the company's size, what's happening in the stock market, the company's potential for short- and long-term growth, and more.

There are two types of stocks you can purchase: common and preferred stock. Both are issued by publicly traded companies (i.e. companies whose stock can be purchased on the stock exchange).

1. **Common stock.** This is also known as ordinary stock. This is the type of stock most people purchase for their investment portfolios. Holders of common stock (shareholders) have certain benefits, like voting privileges where they can vote to elect a company's board of directors or vote on changes to corporate policy. The number of votes they can make depends on the number of shares they own. In addition, shareholders might receive dividends depending on the company's profitability in a given quarter or year and are provided with the company's annual report, which keeps shareholders informed about the company's performance.

2. **Preferred stock.** Preferred stock has certain advantages over common stock in that preferred stock owners have a greater claim to the company's assets and typically earn a fixed dividend payment regardless of how the company is performing. In addition, if the company goes bankrupt, preferred stockholders get paid before common stockholders. However, preferred stock also has its own disadvantages. For instance, preferred stockholders have very limited or no voting rights. Also, a fixed dividend may actually limit the value of their stocks, for example, if the company is performing much better than the value of the fixed dividend the preferred shareholder is receiving.

Based on the differences between the two types of stocks, you assume more risk as a holder of common stock but stand to gain considerably more than preferred stockholders when the company is doing well and growing.

As mentioned earlier on, companies sell stock to raise capital from investors in order to grow their businesses. You buy their stock and in return they incentivize you by aiming to improve the value of the stock by growing the business. As an added bonus, some companies will even pay out dividends tied to their performance and profitability.

## MARKET CAPITALIZATION AND STOCKS

If you read or listen to any financial news, you've probably heard the terms *market capitalization* or *market cap*. One way companies are assessed is through their market capitalization. It is essentially the total market value of a company's outstanding shares (which are the stocks currently held by shareholders), and it is calculated by multiplying a company's outstanding shares by the company's stock price per share. This number is used to assess a company's size and value simply based on its sales or assets. Let's look at an example based on a fictional company that I'll call Bola's Tea Shop. Bola's Tea Shop is publicly traded on the New York Stock Exchange, so investors are able to buy and sell shares in the company. Let's say the tea shop has 200,000 shares available for investors to buy or sell, and the price of each share is $65. If we multiplied the total number of outstanding shares (200,000) by the stock price per share ($65), we come up with $13,000,000, which essentially is the market capitalization of Bola's Tea Shop.

Investopedia.com provides a really good illustration of how market capitalization can be leveraged by investors:

> Using market capitalization to show the size of a company is important because company size is a basic determinant of various characteristics in which investors are interested, including risk. It is also easy to calculate. A company with 20 million shares selling at $100 a share would have a market cap of $2 billion. Given its simplicity and effectiveness for risk assessment, market cap can be a helpful metric in determining which stocks you are interested in, and how to diversify your portfolio with companies of different sizes.[1]

Based on market capitalization, companies are typically broken into large-cap, midcap, and small-cap companies.

**Large-cap companies:** These are companies with market caps of $10 billion or above. They are considered more stable and less risky, especially during and after recessions. Examples of popular large-cap companies at the time of this writing include Walmart, Apple, and Google.

**Midcap companies:** These are companies with market caps between $2 billion and $10 billion. They have high potential for growth and as such are deemed riskier. Examples of popular midcap companies at the time of this writing include Mattel (the toy makers—hey, Barbie!), Dunkin' Brands Group Inc. (which

---

[1]https://www.investopedia.com/terms/m/marketcapitalization.asp.

owns Dunkin' Donuts), and Fair Isaac Corporation (FICO—sound familiar?).

**Small-cap companies:** These are companies with market caps that are less than $2 billion. In some cases, these are younger companies relative to midcap and large-cap ones. They often have large growth potential and are considered higher-risk, but as a result they also have the potential to deliver high returns to investors. Examples of popular small-cap companies at the time of this writing include 1-800-Flowers.com (known for their florals and specialty gift baskets) and Fitbit (known for their smartwatches and devices).

When thinking about your stock investing strategy, it's all about having wide variety and a good balance of stocks from companies with various market capitalizations.

## INVESTING IN BONDS

A bond is basically an IOU (I owe you). It is a loan that you as an investor can make to the government, a corporation, or an organization to help them raise money. In exchange, you'll receive earnings based on the interest payments they promise you for the money you loaned them over a specified term. The type of bond issued depends on the entity issuing the bond. With bonds, you face the risk of losing money if the entity in question is unable to pay you back in full or if you cash out your bond investment before the bond term agreement expires. However, bonds are graded by risk, which can help you make smart decisions when it comes to buying them.

## WHAT TO KNOW ABOUT BONDS

Here are a few terms associated with bonds that are good for you to be familiar with:

- **The borrower or bond issuer.** This is the entity that issues the bond.

- **Interest.** This is the fee the bond issuer pays for what they borrowed. Interest rates can vary across bonds depending on the risk level of the bond, the time until its maturity, and the current market interest rates.
- **Face value.** This is the full amount borrowed.
- **Maturity date.** This is the specific date for eligibility to get the face value back.

Most individual bonds have a face value of $1,000. Bond interest payments happen in advance of you receiving your face value back. Just like with stocks, there are also different types of bonds in the United States. They include:

1. **U.S. government bonds.** These are bonds that are sold by the government to help pay down the national debt and for other federal government projects, like infrastructure, and so on. Bonds issued by the federal government are exempt from state and local income taxes and are further broken into two types:

   - **Treasury bonds and Treasury notes.** Treasury bonds pay interest every 6 months and have 30-year maturities while Treasury notes pay interest every 6 months but have maturity dates of 2 to 10 years.

   - **U.S. savings bonds.** While U.S. savings bonds don't make regular interest payments, they can be purchased at less than their face value. The advantage to this is that you can get the full face value when you cash them in at their maturity date. So, for example, you can buy a U.S. savings bond for $50 that has a face value of $100. There are also different types of savings bonds: **Series EE bonds**, which offer tax breaks when used for higher education, and **Series I bonds**, which provide protection against inflation by increasing the interest rate as inflation rises.

2. **Municipal bonds.** These are bonds used to fund state and local government projects like building schools, hospitals, and roads in cities. They are typically exempt from federal and state income taxes.

3. **Corporate bonds.** These are bonds issued by companies. They typically pay higher interest rates than government bonds, but they're also higher-risk, because if the company goes out of business, it may not be able to pay the interest or face value on the bond. Corporate bonds are also subject to federal and state income taxes.

Speaking of a bond's risk assessment, as defined by The Motley Fool,[2]

> A bond rating is a rating that independent agencies issue to measure the credit quality of a particular bond. The bond rating measures the financial strength of the company issuing the bond, and its ability to make interest payments and repay the principal of the bond, when due.

Here is a bond rating chart based on ratings from two major financial authorities in assessing bond risk (Moody's and Standard & Poor's):

| Bond Rating Chart | | | |
|---|---|---|---|
| Moody's | Standard & Poor's | Grade | Risk |
| Aaa | AAA | Investment | Lowest Risk |
| Aa | AA | Investment | Low Risk |
| A | A | Investment | Low Risk |
| Baa | BBB | Investment | Medium Risk |
| Ba, B | BB, B | Junk | High Risk |
| Caa/Ca/C | CCC/CC/C | Junk | Highest Risk |
| C | D | Junk | In Default |

*Chart source:* https://www.investopedia.com/ask/answers/09/bond-rating.asp.

---

[2]https://www.fool.com/knowledge-center/what-is-a-bond-rating.aspx.

Investment-grade bonds are seen as stable, less risky bond investments and are typically tied to big corporations or government entities. Junk-grade bonds, on the other hand, are bonds that are seen are high-risk, unstable investments by companies who are having issues keeping up with their liabilities. A brokerage platform with research capabilities will show you bonds by rating when you look them up by their company ticker.

---

**In Canada**

In Canada, all levels of government—municipal, federal, and provincial—issue government bonds. In addition to municipal, federal, and provincial bonds, corporate bonds are also available for purchase.[3] A great resource to learn more about the different types of Canadian bonds, how they work, and where to buy them is on the website GetSmarterAboutMoney.ca (https://www.getsmarteraboutmoney.ca/invest/investment-products/bonds/).

**Outside the U.S. or Canada**

You can learn more about bonds offered in your country from a local bank or brokerage or by speaking with a licensed financial advisor in your location.

---

## SHOULD YOU BUY INDIVIDUAL STOCKS AND/OR BONDS?

Now that you have some insight into stocks and bonds as investment types, you should know that you don't have to buy them one by one. You also have the option of effectively buying many stocks or bonds at once by investing in funds.

As we'll go over next, funds provide a simpler way to make sure your money is well-diversified. Buying individual stocks

---

[3]https://www.investright.org/investing-101/types-of-investments/bonds/.

and bonds is often more risky due to less diversification, unless you're individually buying hundreds of different stocks across different company types and industries (which is more labor-intensive and expensive if your brokerage charges a fee per purchase).

If you are new to investing or prefer an easier, more hands-off approach, then investing with built-in variety and diversification is the way to go and starting out with funds is a great idea.

## INVESTING IN FUNDS

Investment funds are pools of money from groups of investors invested in a variety of different stocks and bonds that make up each fund. There are a few different types of funds, including mutual funds, index funds, and exchange-traded funds (ETFs). Let's take a closer look at each one:

- **Managed mutual funds.** A mutual fund is a pool of money from a group of investors set up for the purpose of buying multiple securities like stocks and bonds, all combined into one investment. Mutual funds are typically managed by a fund manager associated with a brokerage firm. Their job is to make investment decisions for the fund and set the fund's objectives, with the main goal of making money for the fund's investors. The active management comes with a price of annual fees that could reduce an investor's overall returns.

- **Index funds.** Index funds are a type of mutual fund, but they are passively managed because they don't need a fund manager to make active decisions about what stocks to include. By Investopedia's definition, "An index fund is a type of mutual fund with a portfolio constructed to match or track the components of a market index, such as the Standard & Poor's 500 Index." In plain English, this means an index fund can be set up to buy all the same stocks within a specific index (like the S&P 500). So, if you were to invest in an index fund tracking the S&P 500, you would be invested in every single one of the 500 companies that make up the S&P 500. You could also purchase a total market index fund, which invests your money in equal ratios across the entire stock market based on a total market index like the Wilshire 5000, which is the broadest stock market index and measures the performance of over 6,700 publicly traded companies. A bond fund is another type of index fund, which invest in thousands of bonds aggregated into one fund.

■ **Exchange-traded funds (ETFs).** ETFs work similarly to index funds and include funds that aggregate stocks or bonds. They are usually passively managed and set up to mimic a particular index. One key difference is that, unlike mutual funds and index funds, which are traded at the end of the day at the market's closing price, ETFs are traded like individual stocks; they can be actively traded throughout the day at whatever the current market price is. For experienced investors trading ETFs, this could be advantageous, as they can track price changes throughout the day and buy or sell ETFs at any point during the day to take advantage of these price changes, which can be pretty substantial. However, with the potential of high short-term gains, there is also high risk involved. ETFs also typically have lower expense ratios than most mutual funds and can sometimes have expenses lower than index mutual funds.[4] However, the fact that they can be actively traded throughout the day means a brokerage may charge commission fees when you buy and sell ETFs, although many brokerages firms in recent times are doing away with these fees.

---

[4]https://www.thebalance.com/differences-between-mutual-funds-and-etfs-2466791.

■ **Real Estate Investment Trusts (REITs).** Another type of investment people like to add to their portfolios are REITs. Basically, REITs are companies that invest in real estate. They make investments in income-producing real estate across different sectors like shopping malls and retail spaces, industrial and office buildings, hotels and resorts, technology and data centers, hospitals, storage facilities, farms, and so forth. Many investors like to add REITs to their portfolios for further diversification and as a way to invest in real estate without having to physically purchase property or deal with property management. Investors in REITs earn a share of the income made from the real estate investments in the form of dividends. Personally, I'm a fan of REIT index funds, which aggregate different types of REITs in different industry sectors like the ones I've just mentioned.

Other key differences between these investment fund types—mutual funds, index funds, and ETFs—revolve around fees and tax efficiencies. ETFs and index funds are almost always cheaper and more tax-efficient than managed mutual funds, which we'll discuss later on.

I'd recommend investing in index funds and/or ETFs depending on your investment goals. If you are unsure, an investment advisor can help you to determine your best option. Personally, my favorite way to invest is in index funds. Let's get into why.

## INDEX FUNDS TO WIN

Index fund investing is a simplified and extremely popular way to invest that is widely leveraged by people focused on building long-term wealth, because it continues to prove itself as a smart way to invest. Index funds were made popular by Jack Bogle, founder of the investment firm Vanguard, which created the world's first index fund in 1975. Jack Bogle's idea behind creating an index fund was that instead of creating human-managed funds to try to beat the performance of the stock market, index funds could simply track the performance of a benchmark index, which would eliminate more of the potential for human error, incur lower brokerage fees, and in turn realize better returns for investors over time. He proved to be right, even decades later.[5]

Across the investment and personal finance world, investing in index funds continues to be a widely talked-about and highly recommended approach to investing. Warren Buffett, one of the wealthiest men in the world as a result of his stock market investing strategies, also loves index funds and has consistently been quoted making statements like, "By periodically investing in an index fund, for example, the know-nothing investor can actually outperform most investment professionals," and, "I think it's the thing (index funds) that makes the most sense practically all of the time." However, to understand why index funds are so popular (and why I and millions of other people are huge fans), let's get into some of their key benefits.

## THE KEY BENEFITS OF INDEX FUNDS

**Index funds are passively managed and as a result are low cost.** As I've mentioned, index funds (and ETFs) are set up to mimic specific indices. Because of this, there is no need for them to be actively managed by fund managers or other financial professionals, as there are typically not a lot of changes that happen in the funds' stock or bond holdings. The average index fund expense ratio is around 0.05% to 0.07% while the average mutual fund expense ratio is around 1% due to their active management.[6] There are even some mutual funds with expense ratios in the 2–3% range. Keep in mind that these expense ratios are charged based on the total amount of money you have invested in your portfolio.

---

[5]https://www.fool.com/investing/2017/06/05/warren-buffetts-hero-revealed.aspx.
[6]https://www.thestreet.com/investing/index-funds-vs-mutual-funds-14836608.

Lower expenses also means larger earnings. You might look at those expense percentages and think, well, it's only 1%. However, the differences in fees can really add up. To put it in real numbers, if you had $10,000 invested in a mutual fund with a 1% expense ratio, you'd be charged $100 in expenses for the year. By contrast, if you had that $10,000 in an index fund with a 0.07% expense ratio, you'd only pay $7. As your portfolio value grows more and more, the differences in expenses stack up as well. Imagine once you have $100,000 invested—it would be painful to pay $1,000 in fees that year instead of just $70! Plus, every extra dollar paid in fees is a dollar that can't compound for you over time. So, expenses can be a big deal.

**Index funds have solid historical returns.** Historical data show that when index funds and actively managed funds are compared, index funds perform better over 80% of the time. And this is despite mutual funds and their managers working hard to beat the performance of the stock market indices. In fact, in a report from CNBC, after 10 years, 85% of large-cap mutual funds had underperformed the S&P 500 index, and after 15 years, nearly 92% were trailing the S&P 500 index.[7] Again, this better performance on average translates into better returns for you as an investor. (Also, better performance for lower fees? Sign me up.)

**Index funds offer great diversification.** Because index funds are made up of hundreds or even thousands of stocks and bonds (often many more than actively managed funds), your investment is very broadly diversified. This diversification helps to reduce your risk, especially during times of market volatility.

**Index funds make taxes easier to manage.** Whenever securities are bought or sold in the stock market, taxable transactions are created. This happens quite often with actively

---

[7]https://www.cnbc.com/2019/03/15/active-fund-managers-trail-the-sp-500-for-the-ninth-year-in-a-row-in-triumph-for-indexing.html.

managed mutual funds. With index funds, trades do not happen as often, which means fewer taxable transactions. If you sell any investments on your own, you'll need to pay taxes on any profits you earned.

## POPULAR INDEX FUNDS

A few examples of popular U.S. index funds from some of the largest brokerage firms include the following:

### Vanguard Total Stock Market Index Fund (Symbol: VTSAX)

- This fund is highly diversified and provides investors exposure across the entire U.S. stock market (over 3,500 stocks).
- Expenses are 0.04%, that is, $4 for every $10,000 invested (as of 2019).
- Its average annual return since inception in 2001 is 7.17% (as of 2019).

### Vanguard 500 Index Fund (Symbol: VFIAX)

- This fund invests in stocks in the S&P 500 Index (a large-cap index).
- It represents 500 of the largest U.S. companies and is considered a good gauge of overall U.S. stock returns.
- Expenses are 0.04%, that is, $4 for every $10,000 invested (as of 2019).
- Its average annual return since inception in 2010 is 6.73% (as of 2019).

### Vanguard Real Estate Index Fund (Symbol: VGSLX)

- This fund invests in real estate investment trusts (REITs)—companies that purchase office buildings, hotels, and other real estate property.

- Expenses are 0.12%, that is, $12 for every $10,000 invested (as of 2019).
- Its average annual return since inception in 2001 is 10.65% (as of 2019).

### Fidelity Zero Total Market Index Fund (Symbol: FZROX)

- This fund is highly diversified and provides investors exposure across the entire U.S. stock market.
- Expenses are 0% (as of 2019).
- Its average annual return since inception in 2018 is 11.05% (as of 2019).

### Fidelity S&P 500 Index Fund (Symbol: FXAIX)

- This fund invests in stocks in the S&P 500 Index (large-cap).
- Expenses are 0.015%, that is, $1.15 for every $10,000 invested (as of 2019).
- Its average annual return since inception in 2018 is 10.50% (as of 2019).

### Fidelity Real Estate Index Fund (Symbol: FSRNX)

- This fund invests in a variety of REITs across various real estate sectors.
- Expenses are 0.07%, that is, $7 for every $10,000 invested (as of 2019).
- Its average annual return since inception in 2018 is 9.93% (as of 2019).

### Schwab Total Stock Index Market Fund (Symbol: SWTSX)

- This fund is highly diversified and provides investors exposure across the entire U.S. stock market.
- Expenses are 0.03%, that is, $3 for every $10,000 invested (as of 2019).

- Its average annual return since inception in 2011 is 6.97% (as of 2019).

### Schwab S&P 500 Index Fund (Symbol: SWPPX)

- This fund invests in stocks in the S&P 500 Index (large-cap).
- It represents 500 of the largest U.S. companies and is considered a good gauge of overall U.S. stock returns.
- Expenses are 0.02%, that is, $2 for every $10,000 invested (as of 2019).
- Its average annual return since inception in 1997 is 8.1% (as of 2019).

---

### In Canada

Some popular Canadian index funds are:

- TD Canadian Index e-series, with a 10-year average annual return of 7.11%
- RBC Canadian Index Fund A, with a 10-year average annual return of 6.64%
- Scotia Canadian Index, with a 10-year average annual return of 6.38%
- *CIBC Canadian Index, with a 10-year average annual return of 6.26%*

*Note:* 10-year average annual return from January 2010 to January 2020.

*Source:* https://morningstar.ca.

### Outside the United States or Canada

To find out what index funds are popular in your country, a great place to start is by performing a Google search for "Popular index funds in [country]" to see what's being talked about and tracked in the financial news and by financial experts.

The main differences between these popular funds are really their expense ratios and the brokerage housing the fund. The average annual fund returns mentioned in the examples are just that: averages. They factor in dips and spikes in the stock markets, recessions, and high-growth years, among other things that drive the performance of the stock market.

# CHAPTER 6

# Researching Your Investments

*Research
is essential
to smart
decision making.*

Before you put your hard-earned money into any investment, you need to do your research. Essentially, you need to understand what you are investing in and determine whether the investment you're considering has the potential for growth. Doing research, however, can be time-consuming and even overwhelming, especially if you are not sure what to look for or haven't done it before. Fortunately, once you understand what to look for, it gets easier to do. Researching your investment is extremely necessary in my opinion and something I highly recommend, even if you are working with the best investment advisor in the game.

Think about it this way: if you were going to purchase a car, it's more than likely that you'd spend time deciding on the make, model, and year of the car you want to buy. You'd probably also spend some time online browsing the Kelly Blue Book website or visiting a couple dealerships in person. And you'd certainly want to see the interior and test-drive the car before you bought it. You wouldn't just go with what the car salesman said was the best car.

Or say you were purchasing your first home. You'd do the research on neighborhoods and the commuting distance from your job or close family members and friends. You'd hire a home inspector to make sure there are no major issues with the systems in the home, and you'd work with your mortgage broker to shop around for the lowest interest rates you could get, right? A home and a car are big purchases, so you are more likely to make the effort to ensure you'll get what you want at the best price.

This same approach should apply to your stock market investments. Over time, your investments can add up to a massive amount of money—money that, based on your objectives, you'll most likely be applying to major life events like your retirement. Thus, it makes sense that you spend some time researching where you invest your hard-earned money so you have a sense of confidence in how your money is invested. Because at the end of the day, clever girls are not about that stress-and-panic life. Especially not because we didn't do our research before we made an investment decision. #thanksbutnothanks

So, let's get into some key things to look for as you begin to research your investments. I'll be looking at both individual stocks and index funds with the examples in this section.

## THINGS TO LOOK FOR WHEN RESEARCHING INVESTMENTS

Before you decide to make an investment, here are five key things you should be looking for that will help you get a good sense of the level of risk associated with each investment and help you make good investing decisions based on your goals and comfort level:

1. The company or fund's financial situation and plans
2. The company or fund's historical performance
3. The company or fund's main objectives and future projections of performance
4. Any associated expenses and/or fees
5. Other considerations, like the company's or fund's leadership track records and media mentions

Let's go over each of these one by one.

1. **The company or fund's financial situation and plans**
   Any company that issues publicly traded stock is required to issue an annual report to its shareholders. These reports include information on the company's financial state, such as its balance sheet (details of its assets, liabilities, profits, losses, and available capital); its revenue and expenses; its short- and long-term objectives and plans for growth; its strategy for navigating competition; and more. Funds are also required to provide an annual report to their shareholders that

discloses how the fund is being operated, its main goals, and its financial state.

These annual reports are available publicly and can be found on the company or fund's website or with a quick Google search. The U.S. Securities and Exchange Commission website (https://www.sec.gov/edgar/searchedgar/companysearch.html) also allows you to access the annual report filings for pretty much any company that is publicly available. Reviewing a company's or fund's annual report, especially its financials, can help you get a good idea of what the company or fund is about and in turn help you make informed investing decisions.

Some more in-depth factors that you may be interested in if you want to geek out when doing your research for a company's stock would include:

- Whether the company owes more than it owns

- Whether the company is reporting profits, or losses (and why)

- Whether they're earning money from their sales and operations, as opposed to having money coming in mostly due to borrowing activities (aka debt)

All of this information can typically be found in the company's publicly available financial reports.

2. **The company or fund's historical performance**
   Looking at historical trends can provide you with important information on how a stock or fund has performed year over year. Essentially, you want to make sure the investment is consistently performing well on average while taking historical economic climates into consideration. For example, the 2008 stock market crash had a hard impact on almost all investments, but some fared better than others. Here are two examples of historical performance charts that are publicly available using an online investment research tool. These two images show the historical performance of Coca-Cola (Symbol: KO) and Vanguard's Total Stock Market Index Fund (Symbol: VTSAX):

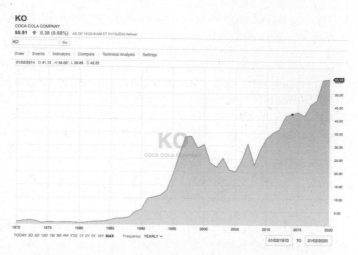

*Source:* Adapted from https://eresearch.fidelity.com/eresearch/
landing.jhtml.

The above image presents a high-level snapshot of Coca-Cola's stock
(Symbol: KO) since 1970. The dips represent market declines, including the
2008 recession. A single share of Coca-Cola stock was approximately $0.88
in January 1970, whereas in this snapshot taken in January 2020 it was worth
close to $56.

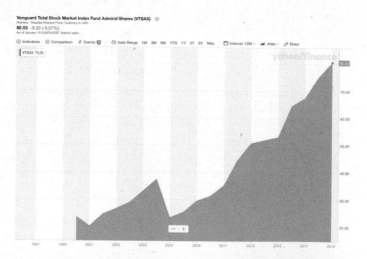

*Source:* Adapted from https://finance.yahoo.com/quote/VTSAX/chart.
The above image presents a high-level snapshot of the Vanguard Total Stock
Market Index Fund (Symbol: VTSAX) since it's been publicly traded starting in
2001. The dips represent market declines, including the 2008 recession. A single
stock of VTSAX was approximately $24 in 2001, whereas in this snapshot taken
in January 2020 it was worth about $80.

3. **The company or fund's main objectives and future projections of performance**

A great place to get a sense for the future projections of your investments is in the annual reports of the stock or fund. As mentioned, annual reports are usually available on the company or fund's website. Some key things to look out for when reviewing an annual report in terms or future projections are:

- What their plans for growth are (e.g. new products, expanding to new markets, acquisitions)
- How their plans will make them profitable
- How they are managing competition

4. **Expenses and fees**

Before you invest, it's important to understand what fees are associated with the investment. That's because fees can eat into your overall returns, especially if the fees are based on a percentage of your investment. Vanguard index funds are some of the most popular in the investing world because of their low fees. Low fees essentially mean more profits for you as an investor. In today's world with high competition among brokerages, and new-age investing avenues through robo-advisors and the like, many brokerages are no longer charging certain fees on many of their investment offerings.

Some common fees include:

- *Brokerage account fees*. This fee type includes things like annual fees to maintain your account and subscriptions for premium account features.

- *Trade commissions*. This is a commission charged when you buy or sell certain investments like stocks or bonds.

- *Mutual fund transaction fees*. This fee is charged when you buy and/or sell some mutual funds.

- *Expense ratios.* This is an annual fee charged by different fund types (not applicable to stocks), which is a percentage of your investment in the fund. Index funds and ETFs usually have the lowest expense ratios.

- *Sales loads.* This is a sales charge or commission on some mutual funds, paid to the broker or salesperson who sold the fund.

- *Management or advisory fees.* Typically, a percentage of your investment that is paid to a financial advisor or robo-advisor.

- *401(k), 403(b), and 459(b) fees.* These are administrative fees to maintain your retirement accounts, often passed on to the plan participants by the employer.

5. **Other considerations (e.g. leadership track records and media mentions)**
When you do your research, it can also help to consider things like track records and media mentions. Looking at the track record of a company's CEO or the track record of a mutual fund manager can provide you with additional insights. A quick Google search or LinkedIn profile visit can tell you about their educational background and investment experience, which is very important given that they are managing millions and even billions of dollars of other people's hard-earned money, yours included. You also want to keep an eye on what's being mentioned in the news when it comes to the company or fund you are interested in, as this could also provide you with valuable insights as you make your investment decisions.

## EXTRA CREDIT: MORE INVESTING TERMS AND DEFINITIONS

There are some additional terms and definitions worth knowing as you start using online research tools through your brokerage firm or on sites like Google Finance, Yahoo Finance, and so on. They include the following:

*Earnings per share (EPS).* EPS is one way to track growth over time. It measures a company's profit divided by the number of shares available for trading. Basically, EPS tells you how profitable each share of a company is.[1]

*Price-to-earnings ratio (P/E Ratio).* This is the ratio of a company's stock price to the company's earnings per share. The ratio is used in valuing companies. This divides the stock's share price by the amount of earnings it has distributed in the last 12 months (per share). A high price/earnings ratio indicates that investors are expecting more growth in the future. Because different industries have different prospects for growth, this indicator is mainly useful when comparing companies within the same industry.[2]

*Price/book ratio.* This is a financial ratio used to compare a company's current market price to its value as entered in the company's books. This ratio divides a stock's share price by the total value of all the company's assets minus its liabilities (per share). If the price/book ratio is low, the shares may be undervalued.[3]

*52-week high/low.* This represents the highest and lowest prices at which the stock has traded in the past year. A stock that nears or passes its previous high or low could see additional trading volume and volatility.[4]

*Dividend yield.* This indicates how much of a company's cash flow is being passed through to investors in the form of dividends. This divides the value of dividends paid in the past year (per share) by the stock's current share value.[5]

---

[1]https://www.investopedia.com/terms/e/eps.asp.
[2]https://www.investopedia.com/terms/p/price-earningsratio.asp.
[3]https://www.investopedia.com/terms/b/booktomarketratio.asp.
[4]https://www.investopedia.com/terms/1/52weekhighlow.asp.
[5]https://www.investopedia.com/terms/d/dividendyield.asp.

*Beta*. This measures how volatile the stock is compared with the overall market.

*Market correction*. This is commonly defined as a drop of 10% or more from a recent high the stock market has experienced. Corrections can happen for several reasons, including changes in the economy or world events like political shifts or pandemics that make investors uncertain, causing them to cash out of their investments quickly. While a correction can cause short-term declines, it can be beneficial in correcting overvalued stocks, allowing for a healthier stock market over time.

The more terminology you know, the more informed your investment decisions will be because you'll be able to more fully understand what you're reading about a stock or fund.[6]

## Take Action

1. Head over to finance.google.com, finance.yahoo.com, morningstar.com, nasdaq.com, or a specific brokerage website, for example, vanguard.com, fidelity.com, schwabfunds.com, and so on. You can pick your favorite based on visual appeal and ease of use, or go with the brokerage firm where you have an account.

2. Under the tools & research section of the site you choose, look up the index funds mentioned in this section and the prior section. You can also look up any other stocks or funds you're interested in to learn more about them and their historical performance. This is your first step to researching an investment!

## CLEVER GIRL INVESTOR: MEET ADEOLA OMOLE

Adeola is a wealth coach, author, and the founder of Millennium Asset Management Corp (adeolaomole.com). She paid off over

---

[6]https://www.investopedia.com/terms/b/beta.asp.

$390,000 of debt (including consumer and mortgage debt) and built a million-dollar portfolio consisting of individual stocks and real estate holdings. Today, she teaches her clients how to manage and invest their money. Creating generational wealth for her family is one of her greatest passions. Adeola's incredible debt payoff story was featured in my first book, *Clever Girl Finance: Ditch Debt, Save Money and Build Real Wealth*, and I'm so grateful to be able to feature her wealth-building journey now.

**Q. You went from paying off over $390,000 of debt to building a 7-figure investment portfolio. How did you do it and how long did it take you?**

A. I paid off over $70,000 of consumer debt in less than three years, and paid off $320,000 that was owed on my home in 12 years. Once the consumer debt was paid off, I made a life-changing decision to aggressively build my investment portfolio while also aggressively paying down my mortgage. It was a bold move that ultimately paid off. I was able to build my investment portfolio by following my Supercharged Financial Strategy. One of the features of this strategy was to divert the payments that were previously going toward my debt repayment, to the creation of wealth. I opened a high-interest savings account and proceeded to deposit the exact same amount of money that was previously being paid to my creditors into this account. The money from the high-interest savings account was used to purchase investment properties, to buy stocks in the equity markets, and to invest in my business. It took me approximately 10 years to reach my goal of amassing a 7-figure net worth.

**Q. It couldn't have been easy; how did you adjust your mindset to stay focused during this journey?**

A. Prior to building my wealth, I had gone through a series of mindset exercises to shift the way I viewed money and investing. Therefore, I already viewed money and wealth from an abundance perspective. This perspective on money and investing helped guide me through my wealth creation journey. I was laser-focused on my goals, as well as on why I was working so hard to achieve my goals. I found myself posting my goals in high-traffic locations throughout my home and my place of work. These gentle reminders worked to keep me motivated to accomplish my bold, audacious goals. That one simple act had such a transformational impact on my life, and served to shift my focus from being exclusively about money to being exclusively about economic options.

**Q. Did you have any investing fears? How did you overcome them?**
A. There was only one fear that I had as it relates to investing, and that was the fear of an investment advisor losing my money. Unfortunately, that fear came true during the 2008 financial crisis. I hired a financial advisor to manage $125,000 of my husband's and my money, and the advisor proceeded to lose close to 75% of the money we entrusted him to manage. That experience strengthened my desire to learn everything I could about self-directed investing. Instead of allowing that experience to deter me from investing in the stock market, I decided to turn the situation around by taking full control of my investment portfolio. I have never looked back, and have been successfully managing my family's investments without the assistance of an advisor.

**Q. Did you make any investing mistakes? And if so, how did you recover from them?**
A. Absolutely! I think every investor makes investment mistakes at the beginning of their investing journey. One of the biggest mistakes I made was not doing thorough due diligence on a company prior to buying its stock. The fact that this mistake was made early in my journey is a saving grace. Had these same mistakes occurred more recently, it would have had a more lasting effect on my investment portfolio. The tip I have for any new investor is not to try to avoid mistakes, but instead do your best to learn from them.

**Q. What is your current investment strategy?**
A. There are a number of investment strategies that I use, but here are the top three:
1. *Value at a deep discount*. I look for value stocks that are at a deep discount to their intrinsic value. These are stocks that have been beaten down due to a host of reasons, none of which has to do with the company's balance sheet.
2. *Mergers arbitrage*. I look for companies that are prospects for mergers and acquisitions and proceed to study their

balance sheet for signs that they may be ripe for a potential takeover.

3. *Early investing*. Finally, I strive to be an early investor in companies that are going to change the way we live. These game-changing stocks tend to be the most rewarding for early investors, but also carry a great deal of risk, as they are often small-capitalization companies that are not yet fully profitable. Game-changing stocks have the capacity to change people's financial lives, as they have changed mine!

**Q. Now that you have established a 7-figure portfolio, what are some of your longer-term investment goals?**
A. I am now on a mission to make my second million. However, this time around it has nothing to do with the options that I will be afforded in life, but instead has everything to do with the options that my children will be afforded in life. Therefore, generational wealth is an important goal for me, and I strive to teach my children how to be good stewards of wealth. As a parent, I have a responsibility to demonstrate through my actions the importance of taking care of one's health and one's wealth. A good friend of mine recently discussed the importance of teaching kids about money, and aptly stated that we need to "teach them the values of how to manage and respect the wealth that we pass down to them as parents." That good friend is Bola Sokunbi, and I personally could not have stated it better myself! Another goal I have is to teach women how to invest confidently in the stock market and options market. I really believe that it's important to share the knowledge that I have acquired over the last several years with as many people as possible.

**Q. What tips would you give to women reading this wanting to accomplish what you have done?**
A. Here are my top three tips for women who want to accomplish what I have accomplished:

1. First, believe that it is possible, and write down the exact dollar amount you want to have. Writing down the amount you want to have has the added bonus of turning a dream into a concrete goal.

2. Now, write down what you are willing to give up in order to achieve this goal. I found that I had to give up certain things in my life in order to accomplish my goal of becoming a millionaire. What are you willing to sacrifice to accomplish your goal?

3. Finally, if you have debt, make a commitment to pay it off, so you can make room in your life for wealth creation.

# CHAPTER 7

# Where and How to Purchase Your Investments

*Be mindful of those investment fees. They may seem small, but they can cost you.*

By this point you have a pretty good foundation of how investing works, so now is a good time to talk about where and how you can purchase your stock market investments to get the ball rolling. The foundational aspect of understanding how investing works is extremely important, but the next most important piece is to actually start investing so that everything you've been learning in theory can be put to work in real life and you can start to earn some real money over time.

Other than choosing investments for a workplace plan like a 401(k), which we'll get to later, the most popular ways to purchase your investments are by:

- **Opening up an investment account with a brokerage firm.** With this route you can start investing on your own or with the help of a robo-advisor, which is an online investment service that provides automated, algorithm-based investment portfolio management advice without the use of human financial planners or advisors.
- **Working with a licensed and reputable financial advisor.** This will allow you to get professional guidance on how to invest your money with the option to have them manage your investments on your behalf.

In the following sections, we'll go over what you need to know about each one of these avenues.

## BROKERAGE FIRMS AND ROBO-ADVISORS

When it comes to buying or selling stock market investments, you are going to need a broker (or a brokerage firm) to manage the transaction. A brokerage firm is a financial institution that manages or facilitates the buying and selling of securities like stocks, bonds, funds, and so on, between buyers and sellers, essentially acting as the "middleman" between both parties. They typically charge commission fees on transactions and can provide you with up-to-date research, market analysis, and pricing information on the various securities you may be interested in purchasing. Examples of large brokerage firms in the United States include companies like Vanguard, Fidelity, Charles Schwab, T-Rowe Price, and TD Ameritrade.

There are three types of brokers that you could leverage to invest in the stock market:

1. **Full-service brokers.** These are basically a one-stop shop for all of your investment needs. They offer money market and brokerage accounts and a wide range of customized financial planning services like estate planning, investment management, and specific individual investing advice via one-on-one sessions with financial advisors, based on your objectives and risk tolerance. As a result of the services they offer, they typically have higher commission fees and other types of service fees (e.g. fees to work with a designated financial advisor), so you need to ensure that whichever full brokerage firm you select is reputable and acts with your best interests as their top priority.

2. **Discount brokers.** Discount brokers offer their services at a considerable discount compared to full-service brokers. Similar to a full-service broker, you can open money market and brokerage accounts with them where you can initiate transactions to buy and sell securities. They are able to offer discounted services because they do not offer customized financial planning advice (i.e. working with a designated financial advisor to develop a plan for your personal situation). However, they do typically have financial advisors available to provide general, nonspecific advice and have human support to help you place investment orders.

3. **Online-only brokers (aka robo-advisors).** Robo-advisors are basically automated online financial advisors that provide financial management services and advice using

algorithms and technology without the need of human financial advisors. They provide customized recommendations of diversified investments based on your individual situation and use software to manage your investments without the high cost of a real-life advisor. However, some robo-advisory firms also provide the option to get advice from a human financial advisor at an additional cost. They typically have very low minimum investment requirements, low fees, regular and automatic portfolio rebalancing, and automated investing, and in many instances they allow you to purchase fractional stocks. Examples of robo-advisors in the United States include companies like Acorns, Betterment, and Wealthfront.

Today it is common to find brokerage firms that provide some or all of these different types of broker services in one place. For instance, many full-service brokers offer discount broker services as well as robo-advisory services. Additionally, many robo-advisory services now offer discount broker services as well. Depending on where you start out, additional broker services might be offered to you as an upsell as your portfolio grows.

Which one should you choose? When starting out with your investment portfolio, you may choose to go with a discount broker or robo-advisor due to the low costs. Particularly for robo-advisors, keep in mind that since their investment recommendations are based on algorithms, they are not financial advisors. This means a robo-advisory firm's algorithm cannot provide you with the level of input that a human financial advisor can provide you if you need to discuss your unique life circumstances or investment objectives. However, as mentioned, some robo-advisory platforms may offer human financial advisory services for an additional cost. Regardless of which service you use, success comes from understanding what you are investing in, being clear about your objectives and risk tolerance, and spending the time to do necessary research to stay on top of your investments.

## WORKING WITH A FINANCIAL ADVISOR

If you decide to work with a financial advisor, it is a decision that should not be taken lightly, because this person is going to be giving you advice and recommendations on financial products and services that can have a major impact on your financial growth over the long term.

According to my friend, Jenny Coombs, associate professor at the College for Financial Planning and founder of gradmoney. org, you want to think about dealing with a financial advisor like walking into a doctor's office after you've done your own extensive research. She states,

> We've all seen the ads on TV or in print showing the picture-perfect work environment of financial advisors and their clients. As soon as you step through the door, you're welcomed like a family member and immediately you have a sense that everything will be perfect. That's a nice image to conjure, but it's part of a carefully crafted script to gain clients' trust and consumers should proceed with caution.

Working with a financial advisor can be a great experience, but it's important that you find the right person who understands your needs and whom you can trust and enjoy working with. To ensure you find the right financial advisor for your needs, you can start by asking for recommendations for great advisors from people you know. You can also do your own independent research by looking up potential candidates on finra.org and on sec.gov; both websites allow you to research the background and experience of financial brokers, advisors, and firms. Once you are comfortable with your findings, you can schedule an initial appointment to get to know the financial advisor and then take an assessment after your meeting to make sure they are someone you would be comfortable working with. Some questions you can ask your financial advisor during your initial meeting include:

Are you a fiduciary (someone who is legally obligated to put your client's best interests first)?

What is your philosophy around investing?

What is your diversification approach?

What is your commission/fee structure?

What qualifications do you have?

What brokerage do you use as a custodian for my investments?

What could my potential tax implications be?

Even if you choose to work with a financial advisor, it's important that you still have an overall financial plan that you are working with (i.e. a plan to pay off debt, save for emergencies, goals, etc.). It's also still a good idea to educate yourself about your investments, because no one cares about your finances more than you.

## PRACTICING WITH SIMULATION ACCOUNTS

As you get comfortable with learning how investing in the stock market works and doing your own research, you may want to consider starting a practice simulation account. Having a simulation account will allow you to test the waters with virtual "play money" you can use to invest in real-time simulations of the stock market. Some great platforms to get started with include:

- Investopedia's stock market game (investopedia.com/simulator/)
- Market Watch's virtual stock exchange (marketwatch.com/game)

With both of these account types, you can test your skills, take challenges, create investment watch-lists, and invest in a variety of stocks, funds, and bonds available for trade in the U.S. stock market.

## TRADING VERSUS INVESTING

I get asked about the difference between trading and investing pretty frequently, so while we are on the topic of how and where to invest, I'd like to touch on this briefly. As discussed throughout this book, the goal of investing is to build long-term wealth by buying stocks, bonds, funds, and so on, and holding onto them for an extended period of time while they appreciate in value and earn returns. With this approach as an investor, your earnings are achieved from compounding, reinvesting your profits, and receiving dividend payments.

Trading, on the other hand, particularly day trading, involves the more frequent buying and selling of stocks over the short term (in many instances multiple times during the course of a day or week) with the goal of generating returns quickly. With trading, profits are made by buying investments at a lower price and selling at a higher price over a short period of time. To summarize the difference between trading and investing at a high level: investing focuses on value and growth while trading focuses on immediate and short-term returns.

Personally, I do not recommend trading unless you are an experienced investor and have plenty of time to dedicate to tracking your investments on a daily or even hourly basis. Trading in itself comes with a high level of risk and requires a specific skillset (which doesn't guarantee success). Yes, some traders make the right predictions, which can make them a lot of money, but the vast majority of traders have high losses even when the stock market is doing great. Furthermore, frequent buying and selling creates many taxable transactions that may come with fees and high tax rates, which in turn reduce profits.

A long-term *buy-and-hold* investing strategy has shown consistently over time that it is possible to earn strong returns when you make good-quality investments. Don't get caught up with what's hot or "trending" or by the quick stock market wins you see others making (and keep in mind that they might not be as public about their losses). Instead, focus on your own long-term objectives and invest accordingly.

## Take Action

Have some fun! Sign up for a simulation account at one of the websites mentioned in this section or on another simulation website of your choice. Even if you are already investing, a simulation account is still a great learning experience. You can use your simulation account to test out investing in any of the stocks or funds you are watching or considering for the near future. (Plus, who doesn't want a hundred grand in play money? It's only virtual money, but it's still fun!)

## CLEVER GIRL INVESTOR: MEET JULLY-ALMA TAVERAS

Jully-Alma Taveras is the founder of Investing Latina (@investinglatina). She started investing as a teenager, made several money mistakes, and then dug herself out of five-figure consumer debt. Now, her mission is to educate others about financial literacy and investing. Her biggest financial accomplishment is investing early with just $50.

**Q. You are a huge advocate for women and investing. What's your personal story and how did you get started with investing?**
A. I started investing when I was 19 years old, right around the time of the historic 2008 recession. While I was in fashion school, I took on a job at a nonprofit organization that focused on providing services to seniors in need. When I sat in the HR meeting to go over the benefits, they highlighted the 403(b) retirement plan and emphasized that they provided a dollar-for-dollar match. All I heard was "free money" and I immediately signed up. I actually made my very first investing mistake two

and a half years later; I left the company prior to having the company match vested. This meant that I lost $6,000 of "free money." Now I make a point to always ask when my employer contributions will be fully vested when I start a new job. Big tip for all of you reading this book!

**Q. What were your fears around investing and how did you deal with them?**

A. Although I didn't have much fear when it came to my 403(b) and 401(k) investments, I became fearful when I was ready to open up my personal brokerage account. I felt a sense of security and comfort with an employer-sponsored account that was actively managed and I trusted was in good hands. But for some reason I was crippled when it came to opening my own personal account. I thought, "What if I mess this up really badly? What if I lose all my hard-earned money?" I was scared, but decided to do it anyway. I realized that if millions of people are investing in the stock market and earning money, then those millions of people cannot all be wrong. If I wanted to build wealth and do something powerful with my earnings, I had no choice but to join in and invest in the market.

**Q. What are some of your long-term goals as they relate to your investments?**

A. My long-term goals include growing my retirement account to $2 million. I am also actively pursuing real estate investing, specifically focusing on a multifamily strategy that can generate cash flow. My goal is to have three to five properties in the next 10 years. Lastly, I'm investing in my business, Investing Latina. I have big dreams of educating girls just like me: Latinas with ambition and the desire to be financially self-reliant.

**Q. What's your current investing strategy?**

A. My current investing strategy is split between retirement, real estate, and business. For my market investments, right now I have 98% of my investments in stocks and 2% in bonds. My stock investments are made up of ETFs, mutual funds, and REITs.

**Q. What advice would you give a woman reading this who might be intimidated by investing?**

A. To any woman reading this who is intimidated by investing, I started with $50, and as I became comfortable I invested more.

That choice I made to invest just $50 was my best financial decision; it helped me develop the habit of investing and paying myself first. Ever since then, I've continued to invest, and I'm dedicated to having a small financial win every day to get me to my multimillion-dollar goal.

# CHAPTER 8

# Investing
# for Retirement

*Living your best life in retirement means planning ahead.*

For most of us, the task of saving for retirement falls entirely on us. Most of us don't have a pension plan, and Social Security (in the United States) is probably not going to provide us with enough money to live anywhere close to a comfortable lifestyle. When it's time to retire, there's no one waiting for us with a mansion on the beach, millions of dollars in the bank, and a bottle of champagne, who's going to say, "Hey, girl! While you were living your best life, I was doing all of this just for you!" Seriously, it doesn't matter how much wishful thinking we do, it's just not going to happen. And so, taking matters into your own hands to save money and invest for retirement is critical.

You may want to retire early to travel more and spend more time with your family. You could do a "partial retirement" where you opt to work part-time or only when you feel like it. Or, you may not be interested in retiring until your later years. Regardless of what retirement scenario you'd prefer, the bottom line is that you are going to need money to live out that ideal and comfortable life in retirement. Personally, I imagine my retirement being fun and stress-free, spending time with my family, traveling at leisure, and living my best life—and I know that "best life" is going to cost me money!

Back when I just graduated from college, I got a short-lived part-time job as a sales associate at a retail pharmacy chain for a few weeks while I was applying to full-time jobs. While I worked there, I met an older lady in her 80s, whom I'll call Anne, who also worked as a sales associate on the same shift as I did. Anne was fun and friendly and always had a good attitude. But she was also extremely slow and sometimes got overwhelmed when there were long lines at the cash register or when she had tons of items to stock on the shelves. I found myself helping her many times to ease her workload. One day, out of curiosity I asked her why she wasn't off enjoying her retirement, why was she working here? She told me honestly that she couldn't afford not to work. She lived alone and needed to pay her rent and buy food. She told me that when she was younger, despite working for many years, she didn't save at all. She didn't really think about it and instead left all financial matters for her husband to manage. When he passed away, she was left with very little money and no assets. Her children were not in a position to help her and she had no desire to be in a state-funded nursing home, and so she was there working with me at that store. It broke my heart to see her struggling with her tasks every day because at her age, she should have been enjoying her retirement instead of standing on her feet for eight-hour shifts helping sometimes rude customers and earning minimum wage. It didn't take long for me to get a full-time job and leave that store, but I took away a valuable lesson—I didn't ever want to find myself in that position when I got older. This is just one example of the importance of saving for retirement as early as you can.

When it comes to retiring early to live life on your own terms, a completely different story is that of my close friend, Kalyn Johnson Chandler, founder and creative director of Effie's Paper: Stationery & Whatnot (effiespaper.com). She was able to retire early as a result of smart planning and went on to start her own business, which she runs successfully today. I asked her to share some insights on how she made it happen. Here's what she shared:

> I started my career as a corporate lawyer at one of the world's largest law firms. To be honest, I decided to go to law school to complement my Master's in Public Policy; I am one of those people who went to law school for the knowledge until I realized how expensive that knowledge was! As a result, I decided to practice law for a few years to make some money and whittle down my student loan debt. Fortunately, a good friend's father was an accountant and financial planner. He sat me down shortly after I started practicing and explained that now was the right time to start saving for retirement. Retirement was the furthest thing from my mind, but I am so thankful for Mr. Piper. He advised me to pay myself with

every paycheck by investing in a variety of mutual funds and stocks of my choosing. I ended up practicing law for 10+ years and was able to save up enough to buy a 2-bedroom condo and sock away a good chunk of money for retirement. When I retired from the practice of law, I had more than enough money to self-fund the start of my company, to live and continue to invest. There's nothing like having your own money and feeling financially independent. One of the best forms of self-care is to pay yourself every pay period. Whether you invest on your own or hire someone to help you, investing for your future is not something to put off until tomorrow.

Then there's my other amazing friend, Yezmin Thomas, an 11-time regional Emmy award–winning journalist, financial coach, and founder of the Smart Dollar Challenge (yezminthomas. com), who started investing early despite retirement being the last thing on her mind. Here's what she shared:

> Fifteen years ago, when I got my first job with benefits, I didn't even understand what a 401(k) was. I asked my husband, "What is a four-zero-one-k?" and he looked at me, confused. After explaining that my new employer was asking me to fill out a 401(k) form and that they offered an 8% match, he knew exactly what I was talking about. "Oh, the 401(k), that's a really good thing; you should max it out to get the match," he told me. That was the first time I ever heard about investing for retirement. It sounded like a good thing to do, to put money away every month before I could even spend it. So, I decided to contribute fifteen percent of my income. Out of sight, out of mind! After enrolling, I forgot about it. It never occurred to me to stop my contributions, not even during the 2008 financial collapse when my husband lost his job and our income went down sixty-five percent. I never want to become a financial burden on anybody. I also love the work that I do, so retirement is the last thing on my mind.

However, investing in my 401(k) is an essential part of my financial plan, because it gives me peace of mind and affords me the luxury to anticipate retirement with excitement. I am confident that the day I decide to retire, it will be on my terms. I am looking forward to spending my mornings enjoying the sounds of nature, drinking coffee on the porch of my farmhouse, reading lifestyle magazines, and admiring the beauty of my horses roaming free through my twenty-acre property in the middle of nowhere. I am going to create this future myself and not rely on the government, the lottery, and most certainly not my kids to support my dreams. By the time I get to retirement age, I would have been investing diligently for forty years to make this future happen. Having that certainty gives you a different perspective on why it's essential to make the sacrifices to invest today in your tomorrow.

Kalyn's and Yezmin's stories are inspiring and quite the opposite from Anne's. However, there are lessons we can learn from all three stories as we plan out our futures. What choice would you rather make starting right now? You might not be in the same position as Kalyn and Yezmin where you started investing early, but the unique opportunity you have by gaining knowledge from reading this book is that you can start today.

Now that I've discussed why saving and investing for retirement should be a top priority, let's get into how to do it.

## TYPES OF RETIREMENT INVESTMENT ACCOUNTS

When it comes to investing for retirement, there are different account types you could have, each with their own benefits and drawbacks. They include the following:

*401(k)—Employer-sponsored.* A 401(k) is an employer-sponsored retirement savings account that only an employer is allowed to offer. Contributing to this account type allows employees to save and invest for retirement on a tax-deferred basis. This means you don't pay income tax on your contributions until you start making withdrawals from your account at retirement.

***403(b), 457(b)—Employer-sponsored.*** Similar to the 401(k), the 403(b) is specific to employees of public schools, certain tax-exempt organizations, and certain ministers while the 457(b) is specific to governmental and certain nongovernmental employers and their employees.

### Benefits and Drawbacks of the 401(k), 403(b), and 457(b)

Benefits

- Many employers will match your contributions up to a certain amount. Matching is a program that some employers offer to encourage you to invest in your retirement with them. When you contribute to their employer-sponsored retirement savings plan, they will match that amount, up to a certain limit, for free. Basically, they are giving you free money for investing in their plan.

- Contributions grow tax-deferred, which means you won't have to pay taxes until you start making withdrawals when you retire. These contributions also lower your annual taxable income during your working years.

- This account type allows for extra catchup contributions if you are above the age of 50.

Drawbacks

- There's an annual limit on how much you can contribute (however, employer contributions don't count toward this).

- You'll have to pay taxes on your money when you retire.

- There are stiff penalties for early withdrawals under the age of 59½.

- These account types typically have fewer investing choices than IRAs.

*Roth 401(k)—Employer-sponsored.* In addition to the 401(k), many employers offer a Roth 401(k) option to their employees, which allows you to make contributions with your after-tax income. It works the same way a Roth IRA does (see overview below), but the main difference is the contribution maximum is much higher, similar to the traditional 401(k).

▶ **NOTE**

Employer retirement accounts are specific to people who have an employer. While many employer plans can have high fees and limited investment options, an employer's plan is sometimes the first exposure many people have to investing. Contributing to these plans allows you to take advantage of any employer match programs if they are offered, or to automate your investing if no employer match exists. In addition, employer plans typically have much higher contribution maximums than other types of retirement accounts.

---

*Traditional IRA.* A traditional IRA is an individual retirement account that allows you to make contributions with your pre-tax income up to a specified amount each year. Come retirement, you will have to pay taxes on any withdrawals you make on the account, just like with a 401(k). An IRA can be set up independently or offered by your employer.

**Benefits and Drawbacks of the Traditional IRA**

Benefits

- Contributions grow tax-deferred, which means you won't have to pay taxes until you start making withdrawals when you retire. These contributions also lower your annual taxable income during your working years.
- You can open an IRA regardless of your employment situation, as long as you've earned taxable income that equals or exceeds your contribution amount for the year.

■ This account type allows for catch-up contributions if you are above the age of 50.

Drawbacks

■ IRA contributions limits are much lower than the 401(k), 403(b), and 457(b) plans.

■ You'll have to pay taxes on your money when you retire.

■ There are stiff penalties for early withdrawals under the age of 59½.

**Roth IRA.** A Roth IRA is an individual retirement account that allows you to make contributions with your after-tax income up to a specified amount each year. Come retirement, your withdrawals will be tax-free, including all profits you've earned. A Roth IRA can be set up independently or offered by your employer.

### Benefits and Drawbacks of the Roth IRA

Benefits

■ Your contributions are made post-tax (i.e. after taxes have been paid on your income), which means there is no deferred tax benefit, but the earnings on your contributions will not be taxed come retirement age.

■ You can make withdrawals on your contributions (just not your profits) before you are eligible without any tax penalties.

■ You can open an IRA regardless of your employment situation, as long as you've earned taxable income that equals or exceeds your contribution amount for the year.

Drawbacks

■ There are income limits determining who is eligible to contribute.

■ IRA contributions limits are much lower than the 401(k), 403(b), and 457(b) plans.

**Simplified Employee Pension (SEP, or SEP IRA)—Employer and self-employed retirement plan.** This retirement plan is most commonly used by small businesses and those who are self-employed (with or without employees), and allows you to contribute up to 25% of your earnings up to a certain amount, tax-deferred. Only employers (including yourself as a self-employed sole proprietor) can make SEP contributions, and each eligible employee (including yourself) must receive the same contribution percentage from you as the employer. A brokerage firm can typically help you set up this account type.

### Benefits and Drawbacks of the SEP

Benefits

- You have the flexibility to choose your contribution requirement depending on how your business is doing, and contributions are not required each year.
- Contributions grow tax-deferred, which means you won't have to pay taxes until you start making withdrawals when you retire. These contributions also lower your annual taxable income during your working years.
- Contributions are deductible on your business tax returns.

Drawbacks

- There are stiff penalties for early withdrawals under the age of 59½.
- You cannot make catchup contributions if you are above the age of 50.

*Solo 401(k) or one-participant 401(k)—Self-employed retirement plan.* This retirement plan is specific to those who are self-employed but have no full-time employees (with the exception of a spouse). It offers many of the same benefits of a traditional 401(k), but with a solo 401(k), business owners can make contributions both as an employee and as an employer, which allows them to maximize both their retirement contributions and their business deductions. This plan also covers spouses who get an income from the business. A brokerage firm can typically help you set up this account type.

### Benefits and Drawbacks of the Solo 401(k)

Benefits

- A solo 401(k) is a great way to contribute for retirement as a self-employed person, as you can contribute more than what is allowable in an IRA.
- You have the choice of selecting a traditional solo 401(k), where you make pre-tax contributions, or a Roth solo 401(k), where you make post-tax contributions.
- You can take loans from your solo 401(k) if needed, although I wouldn't recommend it.
- This account type allows for catchup contributions if you are above the age of 50.

Drawbacks

- You cannot contribute to this plan if you have full-time employees.
- You cannot contribute to this plan if you are already contributing to a 401(k) with an employer, for example, if you have a side hustle where you are self-employed but are also still working full-time and contributing to an employer's plan.

▶ **NOTE**

You can find out more about the various retirement account types, eligibility, and contribution limits on the IRS website (IRS.gov).

---

*Non-retirement accounts.* These are accounts that you can set up independent of any employer. You can save for retirement in non-retirement accounts by leveraging a brokerage account where you invest your after-tax money. While non-retirement accounts do not have the tax benefits of retirement accounts, you'll still be saving money. Because you've already paid taxes on your deposits when you make them, you'll only be required to pay taxes on your earnings when you sell assets at a profit (capital gains) and there are no withdrawal penalties. So, while you don't benefit from the tax shelter, you also don't have to wait until age 59½ to take out your money.

---

**In Canada**

Canada provides tax-advantaged retirement accounts for individuals, including options for those who are self-employed. They include the Canadian Registered Retirement Savings Plan (RRSP, similar to the U.S. traditional IRA), Tax-Free Savings Account (TFSA), and pension plans.[1]

Here's a brief overview of the Registered Retirement Savings Plan (RRSP) and the Tax-Free Savings Account (TFSA):

**The Registered Retirement Savings Plan (RRSP)**

■ The Registered Retirement Savings Plan (RRSP) is a savings plan that is similar to a traditional IRA in the sense that it is not associated with being an employee of a company or public organization (government or nonprofit).

■ Anyone can open up an RRSP at a registered Canadian bank, there are annual contribution limits, and contributions are tax-deductible.

■ RRSPs can hold any type of investments—stocks, bonds, mutual funds, and ETFs, to name a few.

■ You are allowed to contribute to an RRSP up to the year you turn 71 years old. You must then convert your RRSP into a Registered Retirement Income Fund (RRIF) by December 31 of the year you turn 71, which is when you are mandated to start taking money out of your RRIF, in accordance with the withdrawal schedule issued by the Canadian federal government. However,

---

[1]https://www.investopedia.com/articles/retirement/11/difference-retiring-canada-america.asp.

anyone can convert an RRSP into a RRIF as early as the year they turn 65.

### The Tax-Free Savings Account (TFSA)

- While the Tax-Free Savings Account (TFSA) is not technically a retirement account, it offers Canadian residents 18 years of age and older an opportunity to contribute $6,000 annually to this tax-free savings account.

- Contributions made to a TFSA are not tax-deductible. However, income, dividends, and capital gains on investments earned within the TFSA will not be taxed.

- Generally speaking, you can hold the same type of investments in a TFSA as you can hold in an RRSP (i.e. stocks, ETFs, bonds, mutual funds, money market funds, etc.).

- Any money taken out of a TFSA in any given year will be added to the contribution room for the following year. So, for example, if you withdraw $500 from your TFSA in a given year, $500 will be added to your contribution limit for the next year, increasing your contribution allowance by the amount you took out the prior year.

- There are no limits as to how much you can take out of a TFSA. However, you'd need to wait for the following year to re-contribute the amount that you took out in the previous year.

You can learn even more about these account types, their rules, and contribution limits on the Government of Canada website at Canada.ca or by speaking with a licensed financial advisor.

### Outside the United States or Canada

If you are outside of the United States, be sure to research retirement account equivalents in your country or speak to a licensed financial advisor.

Now that you know more about the different types of retirement accounts, you can decide which is right for you. Like the sound of more than one? It's possible to have a combination of these different retirement avenues, depending on your eligibility. You can find out about your eligibility on the IRS website (IRS.gov).

## WHAT TO DO WHEN YOU LEAVE YOUR EMPLOYER

In today's working world, most people no longer stay at their jobs for their entire working careers. As a matter of fact, according to a survey done on Baby Boomers by the Bureau of Labor Statistics, the average worker has had 12.3 different jobs between the ages of 18 and 52, and that number is only expected to keep growing for Millennials and Gen Z.[2] Each time you switch jobs, it's quite common to contribute to a new retirement plan as well. When you're leaving an employer whose plan you have contributed to, you want to ensure that you take your money with you when you leave so you can continue saving effectively for retirement. This is called a rollover.

When you leave a job, you can roll over your money in your former employer's plan into an independently established rollover IRA at a brokerage firm of your choosing. The nice thing about having the money in your own IRA is that you can then invest more cost-effectively with much lower fees and with more transparency than your former employer's plan may have had. Moving your retirement savings into an account outside of your former employer will give you access to the entire stock market. Plus, many employers charge maintenance fees for maintaining former employees' accounts, and these fees can add up, so you definitely don't want to leave your money there.

**What about rolling your money over into your new employer's plan?** Many companies will allow you to do a retirement plan rollover, where you can move your retirement savings from your former employer's plan into the new

---

[2]https://www.bls.gov/news.release/nlsoy.nr0.htm.

employer's plan. However, if you are changing jobs, it's better to move your retirement savings into your own IRA account with a brokerage where you have access to the entire stock market and potentially much lower fees as opposed to moving your money into your new employer's plan.

It's important to keep in mind that transferring the funds into a non-retirement investment account will be considered an early withdrawal and those distributions, if made from pre-tax accounts, will be subject to income taxes and an early-withdrawal penalty. Be sure to review the IRS website (IRS.gov) for qualification requirements and specifics on rules, restrictions, penalties, and exemptions. Transferring it to another retirement account (e.g. a 401(k) to an IRA, or a Roth 401(k) to a Roth IRA) is your best bet for a simple rollover.

## TIPS TO MAXIMIZE YOUR RETIREMENT INVESTMENTS

As you invest for retirement, here are some key steps you should consider taking to ensure you have the nest egg of your dreams:

**Take full advantage of your employer's match if they offer one.** If your employer offers a match, take full advantage of it by contributing enough to get the full match. Otherwise you'll be leaving free money on the table, and nothing beats free money.

**Start contributing toward your retirement savings as soon as you can.** Time is your best friend when it comes to building long-term wealth, especially for retirement. Thanks to the power of compounding, the sooner you start, the more money you'll have come retirement. Starting later? You'll need to be willing to play some catchup and make the extra effort by saving and investing more. This might mean stepping outside of your comfort zone by getting a better-paying job, adding a part-time job, or starting a side hustle to increase your income.

**Max out your contributions if possible.** Not only will maxing out your annual contributions give you an annual tax break (since contributions to traditional plans are pre-tax, i.e. 401(k), 403(b), 457(b), traditional IRA), it will also get you closer to your retirement savings goals. If you are unable to max out your contributions right away, that's okay. Start with small increments of a percentage or two every quarter or every six months.

**Diversify your retirement investments.** It's all about choosing a mix of investments that can help you maximize your returns while still mitigating risk. Don't put all your money into one stock (including your company stock!), since doing this greatly amplifies your risk.

**Roll over your investments when you leave your employer if you participate in their plan.** If you are switching jobs, it's better to move your retirement savings into your own IRA with a brokerage firm. This way you have more investment options and can avoid high fees.

**Don't borrow or withdraw from your retirement savings.** Does your employer give you the option to borrow from your retirement savings account? While this may sound like a great option, don't get too excited yet; when you look at it closely, it might not be such a great idea. Withdrawing or borrowing money from your retirement savings can have adverse effects on your wealth-building efforts over the long term for a number of reasons:

- Like many people who borrow from their retirement accounts, you might have to reduce or stop your new contributions amounts altogether in order to be able to make the loan repayments.
- You will lose the potential long-term gains/earnings you would get if your money had remained invested and was working for you.

- You will lose out on the effects of compounding when you take money out of your retirement savings accounts.
- If you quit or get fired while you have a loan pending from your retirement account, you will have to repay it in full almost immediately; otherwise you will have to pay an early withdrawal penalty.
- If you withdraw your money before your eligible retirement age (e.g. cashing out when you leave a company or from an IRA), you will be liable to pay income taxes as well as an additional 10% penalty on the total amount withdrawn.
- If you are making a withdrawal from a non-taxable retirement account like a Roth IRA, you will still be liable for income tax on your earnings as well as a possible penalty based on the total amount withdrawn (although you can withdraw the amount you've contributed without penalty).

What does this look like in actual numbers? Let's say that right now you are considering taking $1,000 out of your pre-tax retirement account as a withdrawal (e.g. from a traditional IRA). Let's also assume that the average return on your investment for the next year would be ~8%. At the end of that year, you'd have $1,080 in your account. In another year after that, based on annual compounding with a return of 8%, you'd have $1,166 from an original investment of $1,000.

However, if you decided to take that $1,000 as an early withdrawal instead of leaving it to grow, you'd have to pay the following (assuming a 30% tax rate):

Early withdrawal penalty of 10% = −$100
Federal and state tax withholding = −$300

As a result, the balance you would receive would only be $600.00. In addition, your original $1,000 would miss out on the potential earnings and compounding over the years to come, so the lost opportunity is even greater.

It could be that you are eligible to take a loan from a 401(k) that you will pay back over time. While you won't be subject to paying a penalty or taxes in this scenario as long as you pay back the loan, it is likely that you'll be paying interest on the loan amount in addition to (again) sacrificing potential earnings and compounding.

However, if you left that money alone for 10 years, the potential future value of your $1,000 retirement savings could be $2,159, assuming an average return of 8% over that 10 years. That's $600 versus $2,159. The difference is major. And this is only based on our example of $1,000. If it was based on $10,000, it would be a difference of getting $6,000 immediately versus $21,590 in 10 years. I'll just leave that right there.

## ARE YOU SAVING ENOUGH?

As you save for retirement, another important thing to consider is whether you are saving enough. Basically, how much do you need to live comfortably during your retirement years, given that retirement can last on average upwards of 20 to 25 years? Here's how to determine your number.

> **Step 1: Determine how much you'd need on a monthly basis to live comfortably in retirement.** This monthly amount should include things like your living expenses, travel, fun, and so on. Basically, add up the cost of all the things—your essentials plus fun—that you'd like to be able to afford for a full life when you are retired. Take the monthly amount you've decided on and multiply it by 12 so you know how much you need each year.
>
> For example, let's say you decide you'll need $4,000 a month. $4,000 multiplied by 12 months comes out to $48,000 a year that you'll need to live comfortably,

assuming this number is after taxes. Multiplied again by 20 years ($48,000 × 20), again assuming the average length of retirement(starting at 65), you'll need to save $960,000 for your retirement. In order to make sure you are factoring in taxes; you'll want to add on a tax rate of at least ~25% to this so you can cover your annual tax obligations when you start to make withdrawals. This would bring the amount you'd need to save to $1.2 million before taxes. Keep in mind that your annual tax rate will depend on how much you withdraw as income from your retirement account on an annual basis.

**Step 2: Project what you are currently saving for retirement now into the future to determine how much you'll have.** How much are you able to save now? Do you anticipate that increasing in the future? You'll also want to figure out how much you *should* be saving on an annual basis to ensure you meet your long-term retirement goal. Your calculations will need to factor in inflation, and you can play around with seeing how potential investment returns could speed up your journey. A good online retirement calculator can help with both of those things. Keep in mind that you may decide not to retire 100% and instead have a part-time job or business. So, in addition to investments, consider that you may have additional income coming in from a job or business.

Looking at things this way can help you understand how much you need to save to live the life you desire. The good news is that you don't have to save every single spare dollar you have for retirement and sacrifice living a good life right now. You just need to contribute consistently to your retirement account and invest your contributions accordingly. Investing over time will allow your money to compound and gain returns in the form of growth and dividends, which means your money is at work and growing; you just need to give it time.

## INVESTING DURING RETIREMENT

While we frequently talk about retiring by a certain age, it's important to keep in mind that retirement is not a specific date or moment in time; it's a period of time that can last for decades. That means when you retire, you won't be withdrawing all your money at once, so your money still has more time to keep growing. You should also be spending less in retirement than you did while working. Ideally, any expenses related to your kids are gone or greatly reduced (e.g. child-rearing and educational expenses), and your mortgage might be paid off. So, your taxable withdrawals and in turn your taxable rate should be lower.

**Withdrawal rate.** Speaking of withdrawals, one way to plan how much to take out from your investments in retirement is by determining your withdrawal rate. Your withdrawal rate is the percentage of your portfolio that can be withdrawn per year, to ensure that you don't run short of money during your retirement years. A simple formula that is commonly discussed to help figure out your withdrawal rate is the 4% rule. According to Investopedia,[3] this rule seeks to provide a steady income stream to a retiree while also maintaining an account balance that keeps income flowing through retirement. The 4% withdrawal rate is considered to be a sweet spot, as the withdrawals will consist primarily of interest and dividends. For example, if you know you can comfortably live on $40,000 a year in retirement, then your goal would be to save $1 million for retirement so that as you withdraw 4% on an annual basis, your account balance will remain relatively steady as your investments continue to make money and you'll have enough to last your entire retirement.

In retirement, you also still want to ensure that you have an investment strategy in place that transitions to making

---

[3]https://www.investopedia.com/terms/f/four-percent-rule.asp.

your investments more conservative as you age. This will help you hedge against major losses in a market decline and keep your mind at peace about your finances while you enjoy your retirement.

## Take Action

Make sure you have a plan to save for retirement:

1. Determine if your employer offers an employer-sponsored retirement account and if there is a match.
2. Plan to contribute enough to get the full amount of the match if one exists. If a match does not exist, it's still a good idea to contribute anyway to take advantage of the pre-tax benefits.
3. Next, create a plan to max out your contributions by increasing your contribution amounts by small percentage increments once a quarter or once every six months.
4. If you employer does not offer a plan or you are self-employed, look into the other plan types mentioned in this section to determine what will work best for you, and open up an account.
5. Determine how much you need to save for retirement and set your annual retirement account contribution goals.

## CLEVER GIRL INVESTOR: MEET FANEISHA "FO" ALEXANDER

Meet Faneisha "Fo" Alexander. She is a Certified Financial Education Instructor (CFEI) and the founder of Girl Talk with Fo (girltalkwithfo.com). Faneisha successfully paid off over $78,000 in debt in less than three years. Since becoming debt-free, she has built a six-figure investment portfolio before the age of 30. Her passion is to help other women learn to make and manage money to obtain their own financial freedom.

**Q. You went from paying off $78,000 of student loans to now focusing on investing and your own business. How did you do it and how long did it take you?**

A. Paying off my student loans was a three-year journey that consisted of a debt repayment strategy, consistency, and sacrifice. From a strategic standpoint, I worked to increase my income by getting raises, selling unused items in my house, downsizing my lifestyle, and getting on a budget. I implemented the zero-based budget approach and used the debt snowball method to pay off my debt. Although I had to slow down midway through my journey to cashflow my wedding, I still remained consistent with making my debt repayments. Ultimately, after getting married, I combined incomes with my husband. Together we downsized even more and put every extra penny toward finishing off my debt repayment. Now after becoming debt-free, our goal is to invest in the stock market and in my own business. Being debt-free enables us to put more money into the market via retirement savings and our own curated portfolio.

**Q. How did you adjust your mindset to stay focused during your debt payoff process?**

A. It all began with relinquishing the idea that debt was an inevitable part of life. The fact of the matter is that it doesn't have to be. Once I realized that and saw others who could serve as a testament to that end, I knew I could do it. I also had to become more concerned about my future. Where I would spend money on temporal satisfaction and enjoyment, I had to shift my mindset to consider how the decisions that I was making would impact the future me. I didn't want the future me to be living paycheck to paycheck and burdened with debt, so I had to make better decisions in the present.

**Q. What are some key factors that allowed you to build a six-figure investment portfolio?**

A few things contributed to my building a six-figure portfolio—specifically my 401(k). I began investing in retirement as soon as I started working. Although I didn't know much about investing at the time, I knew that I needed to start putting something away for retirement. When I first began, it was simply enough to get the company match; however, after working a few years I paused my contributions to pay off debt. Because of this, I knew

I would have to be a bit more aggressive to make up for the lost time. After paying off my debt, I simply began putting 15% of my income into my retirement savings. This is a general rule of thumb to use to obtain at least one million in retirement savings by age 65. So, although I didn't have a target number in mind for how much I wanted to put away each year, as I received raises and bonuses at work, the amount naturally increased. By being consistent with this, I was able to hit six-figures in retirement savings by age 30. I don't touch my retirement savings, so it simply grows with the market. In addition to my 401(k), my husband and I have an investment portfolio that is just as successful. Contrary to the retirement portfolio, we occasionally do sell shares and use the earnings to cover additional "fun" expenses and purchases. Ultimately, the goal for this portfolio is for it to pay for the "nice to haves" in our lives, possibly fund real estate investments, and make working optional. It's important to note that the success of any portfolio depends on the market, so it can all vary. Nonetheless, with consistent contributions and the right strategy, it's destined to grow.

### Q. What is your current investing approach?

A. I invest 15% of my income into my 401(k), my husband and I invest a portion of our after-tax income into the stock market for non-retirement expenditures, and we plan to begin investing in real estate after paying off our primary residence. To provide additional details, my current strategy, outside of my 401(k), is value investing. Some would call it the Warren Buffett way of investing. Having an employer-provided 401(k) obviously limits your options for investing, so my 401(k) investing strategy is pretty set based on my retirement age target date. However, for investments outside of retirement, we set aside a portion of our income each year to put into the stock market. We typically buy more of the stocks that we already have and, on occasion, introduce some new companies into our portfolio. We utilize an online broker to make all of our investment transactions.

### Q. How would you describe your risk tolerance?

A. I'd say that I'm risk-averse. My husband and I manage our portfolio together and our strategy is to buy and hold. We don't trade and tend to go for companies within industries that we know and that have longevity.

**Q. What tips would you give to women reading this wanting to get started with investing?**

A. My advice would be to first create a plan to manage the funds that you currently have. Get on a budget, get out of debt, save, and then create a plan to start investing. Do your research on which style of investing is best suited to your financial goals. Set aside a small amount of money to get started with. Also, take advantage of free websites that offer simulations for purchasing stocks. Ultimately, gain as much knowledge as you can. More importantly, put that knowledge into action. Nothing will happen until you decide and then take action.

# CHAPTER 9

# Simple Investing Strategies

*Clever girls know . . . sometimes simple strategies are the best strategies.*

To invest successfully, you need to have a plan of action in place to help you achieve your desired financial outcomes. Having a strategy essentially means creating a roadmap to achieve success with your investments. This applies to how you structure your investment portfolio, how you set up your objectives, and how you determine your timeline. Having a strategy will also help you determine how you buy investments and when you sell them according to your goals and objectives. On the flipside, not having a strategy can be equated to driving with a blindfold on, and you absolutely don't want to do that. You want to set a clear path ahead of you and then enjoy the ride while you travel to your destination. Even if it gets bumpy at times, you'll know that with a solid plan in place, just like having a car with great safety features, you'll get to your destination just fine.

So, let's talk strategies. There are several different investing strategies out there. An investment strategy could include trying to do things like:

- Buying investments that are undervalued and holding onto them until they increase in value
- Investing in companies that pay out income in the form of dividends and do so consistently over time
- Investing in companies with growth potential based on revenue and profit forecasts
- A combination of the above and/or other strategies

However, combining or pursuing multiple investment strategies can come with different levels of unnecessary complexity and can require a lot of time because constant research is needed to evaluate each individual company for things like pricing, dividends, and growth potential.

Personally, I prefer simplified and easy-to-manage investment strategies, specifically, strategies that involve index fund portfolios like the 1-fund portfolio, the 2-fund portfolio, the 3-fund portfolio, the 4-fund portfolio, and the 5-fund portfolio investing strategies. These are popular strategies that many investors leverage and love. Let's get into them, starting with the most popular—the 3-fund portfolio.

## THE 3-FUND PORTFOLIO INVESTING STRATEGY

The 3-fund portfolio is basically a portfolio that contains three asset types and uses low-cost index funds or ETFs. In the United States, these three asset types are U.S. stocks, U.S. bonds, and international stocks. Jack Bogle, the founder of the Vanguard brokerage firm, was the first to introduce the idea of index fund investing with the first stock index fund.[1] He then later introduced a bond index and international index to provide his investors with more diversification and more variety of asset classes. Based on these three funds, the 3-fund investing portfolio was born and made popular by the Bogleheads (bogleheads.org), a forum of investing enthusiasts, named to honor Jack Bogle.[2]

The Vanguard funds that are widely considered best for a three-fund portfolio are:[3]

- Vanguard Total Stock Market Index Fund (VTSAX)
- Vanguard Total International Stock Index Fund (VTIAX)
- Vanguard Total Bond Market Fund (VBTLX)

The 3-fund portfolio investing strategy is great for anyone looking for simplicity with investing and a low time commitment.

---

[1] https://en.wikipedia.org/wiki/John_C._Bogle.
[2] https://www.bogleheads.org/wiki/The_Bogleheads%C2%AE.
[3] https://www.bogleheads.org/wiki/Three-fund_portfolio#Choosing_your_asset_allocation.

This is because you simply pick three low-cost funds and then align your investments to your investing objectives, rebalancing your portfolio over time as necessary. Among the benefits of the 3-fund portfolio are the following:

**Great diversification.** Due to the variety of asset classes across a 3-fund portfolio, there's a high level of diversification, which means a lower level of risk and a high chance of your being able to achieve your investment goals when you leverage this investing strategy.

**Low cost.** The expense ratios associated to index funds and ETFs are typically the lowest across the various investment types, including actively managed mutual funds. Because the fees are low, you'll have more money to invest and in turn more money that has the opportunity to grow, as opposed to paying high fees, which over time can have a massive effect on the returns in your portfolio.

**Easy to manage.** Because this strategy has only three funds, it's easy to manage any changes you need to make (e.g. making contributions or withdrawals, updating beneficiaries, tax planning, etc.) and also easy to rebalance your portfolio based on your ideal asset allocation as you achieve your investment goals.

**No advisor or fund manager risk.** When it comes to this strategy you typically don't need a financial advisor, as you're managing your own investments. This means you can save more money and can avoid any conflict-of-interest issues. You can also avoid any issues with fund managers trying to outperform the stock market or making poor investment decisions that you are not aware of.

**Better than average performance.** History has shown that over the long term, index funds outperform actively managed funds. This is because index funds simply follow index benchmarks to track the performance of the stock market (or a particular sector), whereas actively managed funds are focused on earning higher returns for their investors by outperforming the market, which does not often happen.[4]

Given these benefits, the next thing you probably want to know is how you can go about structuring a 3-fund portfolio, or in other words, how you should determine your asset allocation. Well, there are a number of ways to do this.

As mentioned earlier, the 3-fund portfolio consists of index funds invested in U.S. stocks, U.S. bonds, and international stocks. If you are early on in your investing journey, you have the opportunity of time to take on more risk and ride out any market downturns and so you might consider a portfolio more heavily weighted in stocks versus bonds. This is because while bonds can be a solid investment, they are typically much more conservative. Where the average return of stocks over the long-term is between 7 and 8%, bonds have typically had an average return of about 3%. One simple way to allocate the investments in your 3-fund portfolio is to use the rule of thumb, "100 minus your age" to determine your percentage of stocks versus bonds. We'll get into this rule in more detail when we cover rebalancing your portfolio in the next chapter, but the way this works is that you simply use your current age as the percentage of bonds you should have in your portfolio while the rest is in stocks. For example, if you are 30 years old, you could allocate 30% to bonds and the remaining 70% to a mix of U.S. and international stocks. This is just one way a 3-fund portfolio can be structured.

---

[4]https://www.nerdwallet.com/blog/investing/index-funds-vs-mutual-funds-the-differences-that-matter-most-to-investors/.

Some other examples of how a 3-fund portfolio can be structured include:

- Having 80% of your investments in a combination of U.S. and international stocks and the remaining 20% in bonds (this 80/20 approach could be considered as aggressive).

- Having your investment equally allocated across U.S. stocks, U.S. bonds, and international stocks, in the amounts of 33% respectively (this equal division approach could be considered as moderately conservative).

- Having 20% of your investments in a combination of U.S. and international stocks and the remaining 80% in bonds (this 20/80 approach could be considered as highly conservative).

The most attractive perks of a 3-fund portfolio are its simplicity, great diversification, ease of management, and low costs. In addition, 3-fund portfolios are well-suited for new investors. If you'd like to take a deeper dive into the 3-fund portfolio, I highly recommend the book, *The Bogleheads' Guide to the Three-Fund Portfolio*, by Taylor Larimore.

## ALTERNATIVE INVESTING STRATEGIES: THE 1-FUND, 2-FUND, 4-FUND, AND 5-FUND PORTFOLIOS

With every investment strategy, there are always alternatives to consider. The whole idea behind considering other investment approaches is to help you figure out or to confirm which approach will work best for you. So, let's go over a few alternatives to the 3-fund portfolio. They include:

**The 1-fund portfolio.** This investing strategy is the simplest of all and involves investing in one single total stock market or broad market fund. This allows you to invest in a diversified mix of stocks across large, medium, and small-cap companies. The idea behind investing in just one fund is that there is a high enough level of diversification across a total market or broad market fund to still minimize risk even though this portfolio may not have a bond investment component to it. Popular total market funds that would work for this model include the following:

- Vanguard Total Stock Market Index Fund (Symbol: VTSAX)
- Vanguard 500 Index Fund (Symbol: VFIAX)
- Fidelity S&P 500 Index Fund (Symbol: FXAIX)
- Fidelity Zero Total Market Index Fund (Symbol: FZROX)
- Schwab Total Stock Index Market Fund (Symbol: SWTSX)
- Schwab S&P 500 Index Fund (Symbol: SWPPX)

**The 2-fund portfolio.** This investing strategy involves investing in a total stock market or broad market fund and a bond fund. If you're looking to add additional diversification and another asset type to your portfolio, you can consider more than a 1-fund portfolio. Adding a bond fund to your portfolio can further help reduce your overall portfolio risk. Since bonds are much more stable than stocks, they can stabilize a portfolio during swings in the stock market. Popular bond funds include:

- Vanguard Total Bond Market Index Fund (Symbol: VBTLX)
- Fidelity US Bonds Index Fund (Symbol: FSITX)
- Schwab US Aggregate Bond Index Fund (Symbol: SWAGX)

**The 4-fund portfolio.** This investing strategy involves investing in a total stock market or broad market fund, a bond fund, an international stock fund, and an international bond fund. If you want even more diversification than a 3-fund portfolio, this strategy adds an international bond fund. While there are not many international bond funds to speak of, a popular one is the Vanguard Total International Bond Index (Symbol: VTABX).

**The 5-fund portfolio.** This investing strategy involves investing in a total stock market or broad market fund, a bond fund, an international stock fund, an international bond fund, and a REIT fund (Real Estate Investment Trust). Again, this is another way to add even more diversification and additional asset types. As discussed earlier, REITs are Real Estate Investment Trusts and the underlying assets in the portfolio are real estate properties—assets outside of the stock and bond markets. REITs are a great way to invest in real estate without having to physically deal with the property or tenant issues. REIT index funds aggregate multiple different kinds of REITs focusing on different property types, for instance, shopping malls and retail spaces, industrial and office buildings, hotels and resorts, technology and data centers, hospitals, storage facilities, and so forth. Some popular REIT funds include:

- Vanguard Real Estate Index Fund (Symbol: VGSLX)
- Fidelity Real Estate Index Fund (Symbol: FSRNX)

(You may also choose to substitute the international bond fund with a REIT fund in the 4-fund portfolio strategy).

The ultimate goal when it comes to investing is for your money to grow. As a reminder, you can build these portfolios with either index funds or ETFs. It is common for investors to use ETFs in taxable accounts due to better tax treatment and index funds in tax-deferred retirement accounts.

> **Outside the United States**
> If you are outside of the United States, be sure to research investment fund equivalents in your country or speak to a licensed financial advisor.

## Take Action

1. Below are some popular funds (also mentioned through-out this chapter) that can be used to construct your own investing strategy, be it a 1-fund, 2-fund, 3-fund, 4-fund, or 5-fund portfolio. Use these examples as a foundation to begin researching the best investment approach for yourself based on your objectives.

2. Keep in mind these are simply examples and it's still very important that you do your research to make sure you understand an investment before you make any decisions (e.g. looking at the fees, historical performance, fund composition, etc.).

### Examples of Popular U.S. Stock Funds

- Vanguard Total Stock Market Index Fund (Symbol: VTSAX)
- Vanguard 500 Index Fund (Symbol: VFIAX)
- Fidelity S&P 500 Index Fund (Symbol: FXAIX)
- Fidelity Zero Total Market Index Fund (Symbol: FZROX)
- Schwab Total Stock Index Market Fund (Symbol: SWTSX)
- Schwab S&P 500 Index Fund (Symbol: SWPPX)

### Examples of Popular U.S. Bond Funds

- Vanguard Total Bond Market Index Fund (Symbol: VBTLX)
- Fidelity US Bonds Index Fund (Symbol: FSITX)
- Schwab US Aggregate Bond Index Fund (Symbol: SWAGX)

### Examples of Popular International Stock Funds

- Vanguard Total International Index Fund (Symbol: VTIAX)
- Fidelity ZERO International Index Fund (Symbol: FZILX)
- Schwab International Index (Symbol: SWISX)

### Examples of Popular International Bond Funds

- Vanguard Total International Bond Index (Symbol: VTABX)

### Examples of Popular REIT Index Funds

- Vanguard Real Estate Index Fund (Symbol: VGSLX)
- Fidelity Real Estate Index Fund (Symbol: FSRNX)

## CLEVER GIRL INVESTOR: MEET JAMILA SOUFFRANT

Jamila Souffrant is a podcaster, writer, and go-to financial thought leader in the personal finance field. She is also the resident financial expert on a weekly segment on News12, the most watched local TV news-station in New York City. Jamila and her husband saved $169,000 in two years and are debt-free besides their mortgage. She is founder of Journey to Launch (journeytolaunch.com) where she shares her journey to reach financial independence while helping others do the same. She is also a mother of three young children and lives in Brooklyn, NY.

**Q. You and your husband accomplished an amazing feat of saving $169,000 in two years toward your retirement. What were some of the key things you did to achieve this?**
A. We decided to make our savings and investing goals a priority, which meant that all of our other expenses had to fall in line. We determined that we eventually wanted to max out our available pre-tax retirement accounts, which would come out of our paychecks. So, what we got as our net pay was ours to spend on our mandatory and discretionary expenses. As long as our mandatory expenses were taken care of (e.g. the mortgage, child care, groceries, etc.) we would then determine what we had left to spend on discretionary expenses (restaurants, kid activities, etc.). The shift in focus on saving and investing first as a priority allowed us to reach our goals of saving that amount of money over that two-year time period.

**Q. How did you decide where to invest this money?**
A. We wanted to max out all of our tax-advantaged retirement options first to save on taxes. My husband has access to two pre-tax retirement accounts as a teacher, a 403(b) and a 457(b), and I had access to a 401(k) through my job. We then maxed out our Roth IRA via the backdoor Roth IRA strategy, which basically allowed us to convert our traditional IRA to a Roth IRA. After maxing out all of our tax-advantaged accounts, we did taxable investing via index funds in non-retirement accounts. We chose index funds because they are simple and have low fees. I wanted to be able to invest on autopilot and not have to pick individual stocks or make things too complicated. Ultimately, we went for the most simple and low-fee options we could find.

**Q. What are some of your long-term investing goals and how are you ensuring you achieve them?**
A. Long-term we want to make sure that we have enough money invested to cover us in our standard retirement years where we won't have to actively work if we don't want to. Right now, we are on track to have enough saved and invested. We made sure we could achieve that by aggressively investing in previous years so that our money would have more time to compound over time. Since we are long-term investors and don't plan to tap into our tax-advantaged investments any time soon, we are comfortable with keeping our money in mostly equity index funds and riding out any market dips. As we get closer to our standard retirement years, we will adjust our portfolio as necessary.

**Q. You have a busy life as a wife, mother, and entrepreneur; what are some tips you used to simplify your investing approach when you were just starting out?**
A. I knew I wouldn't have a lot of time to sit and research individual companies and stock performances. I wanted something simple and direct, which is why I love index funds. I don't need to beat or outsmart the market, so realizing that for me was key. I didn't overthink my decisions and also know that any investment decision that I make can change as I evolve and learn. So overall, the tips I live by are to keep it simple and just start, because there's no need to overcomplicate things and you won't learn until you take action.

**Q. What advice would you have for women in relationships working on joint investing goals with their partners?**
A. Have real and open conversations about each other's goals. Come together and decide what goals you have as a family and find the middle ground on the best approach. It's also okay to set individual goals apart from your combined family goals but you want to talk about them. Find ways to communicate with each other about the reason or motivation behind your preferences and know that it's okay if you need to have multiple conversations. Also don't be afraid as a woman to speak up and let your voice be heard. Even if your partner has previously taken on the role as the one who is good at money or investing, you have just as much of a say and are equally capable to lead your household on investing and money decisions.

CHAPTER **10**

# Keeping Your Investments on Target

*Rebalancing your portfolio allows you to pause, assess, and simplify.*

As you invest your money over time and work on achieving your financial goals, you'll need to monitor your portfolio and rebalance it as necessary. Rebalancing your portfolio is all about checking in on your investments periodically to ensure your asset allocations are in line with your objectives and you are comfortable with the performance of your investments. It's important to keep in mind that rebalancing your portfolio should be part of your long-term investing strategy. Investing requires patience and as you practice patience over the long term, you might find your portfolio going through short-term swings and declines that periodic rebalancing can help you minimize.

My friend, Nicole Hatcher of frugalchiclife.com, has an excellent take on why patience is key:

> Patience is one of the most important skills to home in on during your investing journey. As female investors, we face unique wealth-building challenges such as the gender pay gap and missed time in the workforce due to childrearing, which can limit our ability to accumulate wealth. Being patient will ensure that we aren't jumping in and out of the market and missing out on opportunities for long-term growth. As an added benefit, being patient and staying the course helps us build investing confidence. It may sound cliché, but it's true: slow-and-steady wins the race.

As you consider rebalancing, remember that you are investing for the long-term and patience is a key factor for your investing success.

## HOW DOES REBALANCING WORK?

How exactly does rebalancing work? Let's say you have $100,000 invested in the stock market and your current objectives involve keeping 70% of your portfolio in stocks and 30% in bonds. You've chosen this investment split because you are looking to achieve growth with your stocks and mitigate risk with your bonds. This equals a portfolio with $70,000 in stocks and $30,000 in bonds. Let's then say that over time, the value of your stock investments double and they are now valued at $140,000, and your bonds are valued at $40,000. Your portfolio is no longer balanced according to your objective, since your stock investments now make up 78% of your portfolio instead of 70%. If your objective remains the same, you'd need to rebalance your portfolio by selling some stocks (– $14,000) and buying more bonds (+ $14,000) to get you back to that 70/30 split. However, if your objectives have changed, and you instead are taking a more aggressive approach to your investing and want a larger percentage of stocks in your portfolio, then there's no action required on your part. This is a simple example of how you could approach rebalancing your portfolio.

## WHEN TO REBALANCE YOUR PORTFOLIO

To elaborate even further, you may want to consider rebalancing your portfolio if any of the following happens:

**Major gains or major losses significantly change your asset allocation.** You'd need to determine how much money you want to have in one asset class, industry, or investment type as you invest. Based on this determination, if major gains or losses occur that change your asset allocation, then that could be a good time to rebalance your portfolio.

**Your financial goals and objectives change.** Perhaps you decide to move your retirement date up ten years earlier or move it out ten years later. You might decide you want to invest for your child's college education or do more socially conscious investing. Scenarios like this might require that you adjust your portfolio accordingly to accommodate these changes to your goals.

**You are approaching retirement.** As you approach your big retirement goal, it's typically recommended that you get more conservative with your investments so that if the market goes through a decline, your portfolio and in turn your life plans are not heavily impacted.

## A COMMON RULE OF THUMB: 100 MINUS YOUR AGE

A pretty common rule of thumb and basic investing principle when it comes to keeping your portfolio balanced that I mentioned earlier is the rule of *100 minus your age*. This guideline essentially helps you to reduce your investment risk as you get older. It works by helping you determine how much you should consider keeping in stocks (including funds) versus how much you should keep in bonds. Going back to the example I used in the previous chapter, if you are 30 years old, then 100 minus your age equals 70. So according to the rule, you should keep 70% of your investments in equities and the other 30% in bonds.

However, if you have a high risk tolerance or lots of time to invest, you can modify this rule to be 110 or 120 minus your age. Basically, this modification means you will have even more money invested in stocks and more of an aggressive portfolio, which could mean larger returns (albeit higher risks). With a more aggressive portfolio and with time on your side, you are better able to weather market declines, as a lengthier investing timeline means more time for the market (and your portfolio) to recover. Again, using the idea of 100 minus your age to make investment decisions is just a general guideline and not gospel. As you make your investment decisions, you always want to consider your own personal objectives, your investing timeline, and your risk tolerance.

## HOW OFTEN SHOULD YOU REBALANCE YOUR PORTFOLIO?

So how often is too often when it comes to rebalancing your portfolio? A good baseline is to review your asset allocations and rebalance your portfolio, if needed, once a year. Rebalancing your portfolio unnecessarily or more than once a year might be excessive if the changes in your portfolio are minimal. It can also get expensive and eat into your returns due to any associated transaction fees and taxes on earnings when you sell your stock market investments.

## TARGET-DATE FUNDS, ROBO-ADVISORS, AND PORTFOLIO REBALANCING

One easy way to get around rebalancing your portfolio on your own is by investing in a target-date fund. A target-date retirement fund is an age-based fund designed to gradually shift your asset allocation over time to fewer stocks and more bonds and cash, so that the fund becomes more conservative the closer you get to your retirement year, minimizing your investment risk over time. If you are invested in a target-date retirement fund, you typically don't have to worry about rebalancing your portfolio, as this is done automatically in the fund each year as you move closer to retirement. However, it's important to keep in mind that target funds are typically actively managed by a fund manager and this means potentially higher fees, which can eat into your investment returns.

Another easy way to get around rebalancing your portfolio is if you have your investments with a robo-advisor that includes the benefit of automatic portfolio rebalancing based on the objectives you specify when you set up your account. You will be able to adjust your objectives as needed and the robo-advisor service will use your selections for future portfolio rebalancing as necessary.

With target-date funds and robo-advisors, you want to make sure you monitor your accounts periodically to ensure your investments are performing in line with your long-term goals.

## LETTING GO OF A LOSING INVESTMENT

Sometimes as investors it's easy to get super-vested in a company because we love their products or services so much, we are going off the company's past glory, or perhaps we just really love the company's founders. However, sometimes we need to let go of certain investments that might be holding our portfolios down. My friend, Jenny Coombs, associate professor at the College for Financial Planning and founder of gradmoney.org, says knowing when to let go of a losing investment is important to the process of rebalancing your portfolio. Here's her take on this:

> I think more tears have been shed over declining stock than cash lost on a hand of poker at a casino. Maybe because one is a long, slow drawn-out process and the other is quick, yet neither is painless. However, sometimes the worst may be over and you just don't know it! Investments go up and down all the time, and unless you have a tough stomach, I highly advise that you only check your portfolio a few times per year to see how things are going. It is normal for a stock to lose value from time to time but in the end with a long-term focus and with patience, you should end up with more than when you started. There are, however, some times when you just cannot save a sinking ship.

How do you know when it's time to give up and take a loss on an investment that's losing you money? Here are Jenny's quick tips:

**The stock or fund reaches your "stop-loss" limit.** This is a very easy way to make sure that an investment will never lose more than you can afford to lose. A stop-loss is a minimum price you are willing to let an investment decline to before you cut your losses and sell it; most brokerage accounts have this ability automatically built-in if you set it up for your portfolio.

**The investment's fundamentals have changed for the worse.** Investments can have adverse reactions to news and earnings events, but that does not necessarily mean that the investment is doomed. For example, If Google's stock or your favorite Vanguard index fund dropped 10% in a day, you would not necessarily think that the investment is doomed, right? Of course not, because it's a stable investment with plenty of long-term growth and their historical performance supports that. Knowing why you bought an investment in the first place is very helpful—it should be because the investment is expected to keep gaining value over time and there is nothing in the foreseeable future that will upset this balance. Understanding your investments is key but feeling comfortable about them is equally important. If management has changed for the worse, the company is continuously embroiled in scandal, or the industry or market segment is declining beyond your comfort level, then it's okay to get out of the investment.

**The company declared bankruptcy**. If you are invested in individual stocks, sometimes there are situations where a company will declare bankruptcy with only a few advance signs. There are two types of bankruptcy a company can file: chapter 11 and chapter 9. Chapter 11 bankruptcy simply means the company will be restructuring and there will be a lot of change happening in the near-term. This is what American Airlines had to do after 9/11 and it got back on its feet. Chapter 9 bankruptcy means the company will completely dissolve its assets and it's pretty much over—get out of this stock as soon as you can. With investments in funds, the good news is that a fund's investments can typically absorb the impact of a company's bankruptcy filing with minimal impact to your portfolio because of the high level of diversification within the fund.

In the end, it's important to remember that selling an investment at a loss is not the end of the world and surely if you keep investing, you will more than make up the difference with big winners in the long run. You can't say that will happen in a game of poker!

## Take Action

1. Set a calendar reminder for every quarter to review your investment portfolio to ensure your investments are performing in line with your long-term objectives.

2. Also set a reminder to rebalance your portfolio once a year if necessary to sell the investments that are putting your asset allocation off balance and then to buy more of what you need to attain the right balance.

3. Nothing to rebalance? That's perfectly fine. If your portfolio remains in line with your current objectives, then you don't need to change anything. It's not necessary to rebalance your portfolio just for the sake of rebalancing—this can get expensive.

4. Not sure you want to do this on your own? Plan to schedule time to speak with a financial advisor who can help you.

# The Deal with Taxes

# Be prepared for taxes.

"**Y**ou don't pay taxes. They take taxes." The first time I heard that Chris Rock quote, it made me laugh out loud #lol. Ever heard the saying that only two things in life are certain, death and taxes? Well, his quote is kind of along the same lines. When it comes to your investments, an important fact you need to know is that when you start to make withdrawals, you'll need to pay taxes, so you want to be prepared for this. This means making sure you build your potential tax obligations into your long-term plans. While the specific details around taxes (especially given constant tax law changes) are best suited for your accountant or investment advisor, I'll be sharing some general things that you can keep in mind.

## INCOME TAX AND CAPITAL GAINS TAX

When you start to make withdrawals from a tax-deferred account like a 401(k), 457(b), 403(b), or traditional IRAs, you'll be subject to income tax at whatever your future tax rate is at the time of your withdrawals. If you make withdrawals from a taxable account like a regular brokerage account, then you'd be subject to capital gains tax on any earnings your investments made. To clearly define the two, income tax is the tax you pay on earnings from being employed, interest, dividends, royalties, or self-employment while capital gains tax is the tax you pay on income derived directly from the sale of an asset, such as a stock.[1] In the United States, capital gains taxes can be anywhere from 0% up to 20%, which is also tied to how long you've held the investment. It is typically less than income tax, which runs anywhere from 10% up to 37% and is assessed based on a person's income and tax bracket. So, for instance, you could be subject to income tax on dividends earned by your investments and subject to capital gains tax when you sell a stock that has grown in value from the time you first purchased it. When you sell stocks

---

[1]https://www.investopedia.com/ask/answers/052015/what-difference-between-income-tax-and-capital-gains-tax.asp.

and make withdrawals from tax-exempt accounts (e.g. a Roth IRA), you will not have to pay any taxes as long as you meet the account type and withdrawal age requirements.

It's very difficult to predict what future tax rates will be, and there is the possibility that they could be higher or lower than present-day rates. If you think your future tax bracket will be lower than what you currently pay, you could benefit from a lower future tax rate by having a traditional IRA. However, if you think your tax bracket will be higher than what it is now, a Roth IRA might be best since you would have already paid taxes on your contributions and therefore wouldn't have to pay income tax on your disbursements in retirement.

That being said, it's not uncommon to have both types of IRA accounts (a traditional IRA and a Roth IRA). If you qualify for both a traditional and a Roth IRA, you'll be able to save more by leveraging the benefits of both of these retirement plans over the long term. By design, once you reach age 59½, you are allowed to begin making withdrawals from your retirement accounts without penalties. You just want to make sure you are aware of the qualification requirements put in place by the IRS, which you can learn more about at irs.gov.

## TAX LOSSES

On the flipside of paying taxes on your investment earnings is the ability to offset and deduct taxes from any investment losses you experience. Capital losses are defined as losses that occur as result of an investment decreasing in value between when you purchased it and when you sold it. These types of losses may be applied toward a capital gains tax obligation to minimize what you might owe. This is also known as tax-loss harvesting and can be enabled automatically with many robo-advisors or done on your own if you are a more experienced investor. However, when it comes to taxes, if your tax situation is complex, confusing, or you are unsure, I strongly recommend seeking professional guidance.

## MINIMIZING YOUR TAX OBLIGATION

While paying taxes is unavoidable, if you can pay less in taxes, then you can save even more and have more money to put toward your financial and life goals. One way to minimize your tax obligations, mentioned already in this book, is to take advantage of tax-deferred accounts. By contributing to and maxing out your tax-deferred accounts like the 401(k), 457(b), 403(b), or traditional IRAs, you can reduce the total amount of taxes you pay over the course of your life.

To illustrate, let's say you are single and earn $86,000 a year living in New York City. Based on your income, and according to the 2020 IRS tax rates (see table), your tax rate will be distributed across multiple tax brackets (which is essentially the tax rate you pay on each portion of your income). On an $86,000 salary your tax rate would be as follows: you'd pay 10% on the first $9,876, 12% on the amount between $9,875 and $40,125, 22% on the amount between $40,126 to $85,525, and 24% on the

**2020 Tax Brackets and Rates**

| Tax Rate | Single | Head of Household | Married, Filing Jointly | Married, Filing Separately |
|---|---|---|---|---|
| 10% | $0 to $9,875 | $0 to $14,100 | $0 to $19,750 | $0 to $9,875 |
| 12% | $9,876 to $40,125 | $14,101 to $53,700 | $19,751 to $80,250 | $9,876 to $40,125 |
| 22% | $40,126 to $85,525 | $53,701 to $85,500 | $80,251 to $171,050 | $40,126 to $85,525 |
| 24% | $85,526 to $163,300 | $85,501 to $163,300 | $171,051 to $326,600 | $85,526 to $163,300 |
| 32% | $163,301 to $207,350 | $163,301 to $207,350 | $326,601 to $414,700 | $163,301 to $207,350 |
| 35% | $207,351 to $518,400 | $207,351 to $518,400 | $414,701 to $622,050 | $207,351 to $311,025 |
| 37% | $518,401 or more | $518,401 or more | $622,051 or more | $311,026 or more |

(*Source:* IRS.gov)

remaining $474. This progressive tax system in the United States means that the more you earn, the higher your taxes will be.

With this breakdown, the total amount in federal income taxes alone on an $86,000 salary would be $12,095, for an average tax rate of 14.06%. While we're looking at federal income tax alone for this example, keep in mind that you'd also pay FICA taxes of 7.65% (this is the same for everyone and does not change by bracket), plus whatever your state's rate for income tax is (and any local taxes as well).

However, if you were to contribute $12,000 to a 401(k), 457(b), or 403(b), your federal income tax obligation would fall to $9,455 at an average tax rate of 12.78%, saving you $2,640 for the year. If you also contributed $6,000 to a traditional IRA, then your annual federal income tax obligation would go down further to $8,135 for a total average tax rate of 11.96%, saving you $3,960 for the year.

Essentially, you're now paying 0% in federal income taxes for the year on that $18,000 you contributed to your retirement savings, whereas before you would have paid 22% on it.

This example highlights one way in which you can reduce your taxable income during your working years, but what about during actual retirement?

In retirement, your annual tax obligation will be dependent on what your annual investment withdrawal rate is from your tax-deferred accounts. This annual investment withdrawal is considered income and would be taxable based on the progressive tax brackets of that year. For example, let's say you retire in 20 years to a less expensive location like Florida and your future tax rate is exactly the same as it is today (see 2020 table above). If you are married and filing jointly and you withdraw $75,000 annually, then your federal income tax obligation as a couple would be $5,684 at an average tax rate of 7.58%, compared to $4,484 (an average tax rate of 6.90%) if you were to withdraw $65,000. Over several years, these amounts really do add up.

You certainly want to enjoy each year of your retirement, especially after working so hard to get there. However, you want to make sure you are withdrawing just what you need in order to minimize your annual tax obligation since the money you save on taxes can stay invested and hard at work on your behalf.

Again, if necessary, be sure to seek professional guidance when it comes to tax-related matters.

## Take Action

1. Determine how you can increase your tax-deferred retirement contributions with a goal of maxing out your contributions in order to reduce your taxable income (and increase your investments). If you are unable to max out at this time, start with small percentage increments every quarter or every six months.

2. Based on the determination you made earlier on in this book of how much you need to save for retirement, be sure to factor in taxes to your plan.

3. Consult with a tax professional if you need specific guidance. Also be sure to confirm the latest tax rates on irs.gov.

# CHAPTER 12

# Investing Mistakes and Pitfalls to Avoid

*Clever girls know . . . mistakes are valuable lessons and learning from the mistakes of others can put you ahead on your journey to success.*

There are a lot of mistakes that investors can make. Sometimes mistakes happen due to poor investment decisions and sometimes they happen due to oversight. If you read my first book, *Clever Girl Finance: Ditch Debt, Save Money and Build Real Wealth*, then you know all about my designer-handbag-buying habit and how I stopped saving as much as I could have and started buying designer handbags that I rarely used. After realizing so many expensive handbags didn't make sense for my lifestyle, I sold them (some at a profit due to the various designers' brand popularity), but I was still disappointed that I had blindly invested in the wrong thing (handbags). I say this because if I had invested that money in the stock market instead, then today I would have over 10 times the money I spent on those handbags. *Hmmm.* Let's not talk about it.

As you go through life, there are also totally unexpected things that can throw you off the path of your long-term goals. Take my friend, Sheryl Hickerson, CEO of Females and Finances and the founder of the Facebook group of the same name, who shared this unplanned life transition that shook up her long term financial plans:

> "I don't want to be married to you anymore." Those are the words my ex-husband said to me after twenty-four years of marriage via mobile phone, not even to my face. I remember driving home and finding our bank accounts were emptied, retirement plans gone, and all my dreams of settling into my second stage of life were finished.

Despite this devastating situation, Sheryl is now in full recovery mode and thriving:

> At 47, I learned two very valuable lessons from this. One, I had left my investments in the hands of someone who was not a financial expert and should never do this again. Two, you can rebuild your investment nest even when you're older, it just takes

a lot of work and smart financial service friends to help get you back on track. Ladies, put your own oxygen mask on first—every single day!

Whether it's a poor financial decision, an oversight, or an unplanned life transition like in Sheryl's case, things can happen that will throw you for a loop. However, I love to look at every single situation as a learning experience. I chose this approach because when I can assess what went wrong and how it went wrong, I can better determine the next best steps to take to achieve success in the future. So, let's talk about some of the most common mistakes investors make and how you can avoid them.

## KEY INVESTING MISTAKES AND HOW TO AVOID THEM

**Waiting to invest.** When it comes to investing, time is your biggest asset and the best time to start investing is right now. By investing early on, you'll have a better chance of greater returns on your investments. Not only will you have more time to contribute to your investments; you will also have more time for your investments to grow and benefit from the "magic" of compounding.

**Investing with emotion.** Watching every dip and climb that happens in the stock market every day is a bad idea and will cause you unnecessary stress. Investing without any research because your best friend or family member recommended a particular investment is also a bad idea. Things like this are recipes for disaster. Why? Because investing requires you to be objective and put your emotions aside. You'll need to ask yourself questions like, Does this investment make sense? Do I understand it? What is the level of risk? What is the rate of return? How much time am I able to invest? When it comes to making investing decisions, it's important to set your emotions aside and make your decisions with a clear head and based on your long-term financial goals.

**Trusting someone else to manage your investments without any involvement from you.** Whether you work with a financial planner or advisor or your partner manages the investment decisions, I can't stress the importance of understanding your financial big picture and being involved in any financial decisions being made. Understanding where and how your money is invested, where the accounts are, what the investment decisions are based on, and how to access your investments is so important. Investing jointly? Make sure your name is on the investments, too!

**Trying to time the market.** This can also be described as attempting to predict the future and buy or sell based on when you think the market is high or low. More often than not, this does not work and can result in a ton of poor decisions and wasted time, both of which can cost you a lot money, so forget about timing the market. Your focus should be on understanding your investments and creating a long-term plan that aligns with your life and your financial goals. Once you have a solid long-term investment plan in place, you can become more conservative as you approach the timeline when you'll need your money.

**Expecting overnight returns on your investments.** There's no such thing as an overnight sensation, at least not literally, and if anyone is trying to sell this to you, run! Grab your handbag, your car keys, pack up your lunch, and get out of there. Investments require time to perform and grow in value and Rome was not built in a day.

**Not considering taxes in your long-term plan.** Understanding what your potential tax burden will be is critical to your plan. You'll need to make sure you factor in how much in taxes you will have to pay on your earnings. This way, you can ensure you are achieving your financial goals from investing in addition to your tax obligations. A financial advisor or a tax accountant can guide you through this conversation around taxes.

\*\*\*

Now that you know what investment pitfalls to avoid, you can revise your strategy accordingly and set yourself up for even greater success with your money over the long term.

## CLEVER GIRL INVESTOR: MEET REGINA BYRD

Meet Regina Byrd. She is a generational wealth specialist. She is also the founder and CEO of Prosper with Regina LLC (prosper-withregina.com) and author of the book, *10 Prosperity Secrets for the Young and Fly*. Her mission is to educate mothers and their teenagers on how to achieve financial independence and create generational wealth. She does this by teaching them how to create multiple streams of income, how to invest to build wealth, and how to protect the wealth that they build. Her biggest reward comes from doing work that gives mothers the tools and resources they need to be successful in life.

**Q. How did investing play a part in your journey to financial wellness as a young woman?**
A. Investing played a part in my journey because it helped me to understand how money really works. Building wealth is more than just receiving a paycheck; it is also understanding how you can take a set amount of money and grow it. Investing opened my eyes to understanding the importance of compound interest and how I needed to allow my money to work for me so I could get to a place of financial empowerment. Investing opened my eyes to the world of how money works, and I have never looked back. When I was younger, I did not invest. Today I do. I'm 34 and I can tell you what I do now. I invest on my own and through my job. My job provides a 6% contribution match for my 401(k). So, I contribute 10% of my income and take advantage of the 6% match from my company. Every pay period, I also allocate a certain amount of my money for investments. I either invest in marketing for my business or knowledge that will yield a return from me applying what I learned in my business. I may also purchase a stock or fund for myself to add to my portfolio. Usually I invest mostly in stocks or funds, but lately I have been heavily researching REITs (Real Estate Investment Trusts) and

have started investing there. Also last year, I purchased my very first home in cash at the age of 33. Even though we currently live in the home, it was purchased as an investment property. We are in the process of fixing it up to rent out soon.

**Q. One of your main goals is building generational wealth for your two children. How are you doing this and what is your current investment strategy?**

A. Yes, we are a doing a number of things to build generational wealth for our children. Our current strategy for them includes life insurance policies with cash value, 529 college savings accounts, certificates of deposit, establishing a trust fund for them, purchasing stocks in their name quarterly, and purchasing a home that will be left to our children. In the future we plan to do more real estate and business investing involving them as well.

**Q. How are you teaching your children to invest and about financial responsibility?**

A. Once a week we have a session at our house called "Money School." Money School is a 15- to 30-minute session where we teach our children different financial topics with the use of a money calendar, flashcards, songs, books, and money-specific lessons. We also utilize the 3-Jar system to teach them budgeting, labeling the jars saving, spending, and giving. In addition, each of our children has stock market investments, so we take turns looking at their portfolio and explaining their profits to them, as well as the ebbs and flows of their stocks. Teaching your children to be financially astute is a lifelong journey that does not happen in one day but over years of consistency, so these weekly lessons are incredibly important to my family.

**Q. You have a big focus on teaching young college aged women how to build wealth with investing—why is this age group a focus?**

A. Well as a young person, you don't know what you don't know. Most young adults and college students are exposed to other young adults and college students, which means most kids are getting their financial advice from their peers. If you are not blessed to have financially savvy parents, and the school system does not teach you about finances, you are left to be taught by the world or better yet your friends. And by that time, most college students have already signed on the dotted lines for student loans and credit cards, signing their future paychecks away at such an early age. It's really sad when you think about the student loan process. Before you even have a job, before you even go to the interview or get a job offer, most students are in debt. This is why it's so important to reach young people early to teach them how to make the best money decisions for themselves. As women specifically, it's easy for us to get sucked into the world of comparison and start doubting our power thanks to social media. Before they reach adulthood, young women must know who they are so they can make smart financial decisions for themselves and not based on how they are being influenced on social media. It's so sad for me to see young girls wasting money on things without acquiring any assets. The world has made it okay to have priorities mixed up. This is why college and high school girls are so important to teach financial education.

**Q. You also work with a lot of mothers, specifically single mothers, on improving their personal finances and building generational wealth despite not having a dual-income household. What are some everyday tips you share to help them start investing consistently?**

A. I would say to them just like you budget your bills, you should budget your investments. Look at investing as another bill that you have to pay in order to ensure the future that you desire. Your utility bills will not make you rich or help you build generational wealth. However, your investments will bring wealth in your life. Make budgeting your investments as important as your monthly bills. Oftentimes people think investing only has to do with investing in the stock market or real estate. Although those are equally important, investing in yourself is crucial. I always allocate a portion to investing in myself and for my children, whether that is investing in a coach, a seminar, or in actual stocks. Another way to allocate money to investing is to automate sending a part of your income to an investment account. You will be surprised that you can "miraculously" find the money to invest when you automate those deposits.

**Q. It's also important to have the right mindset about investing; what would you say to someone just getting started?**

A. I would say start where you are. Please do not think that because you do not have a lot of money, you should not invest.

It is actually the total opposite; because you do not have a lot of money, you should invest so your money can grow. Start with what you have, even if that means starting with $5. There are so many apps that you can use to start investing. Also don't play the short game; investing is a long-term strategy with great rewards. In the wise words of Warren Buffett, "Nobody wants to get rich slow," but if you follow this approach, you will.

# In Closing

# No one can care about your financial wellness more than you.

Congratulations! You've made it to the end of this book, and my hope is that you feel a higher level of confidence as you approach investing. That being said, here are some key takeaways to keep in mind now that you've gotten to this point.

## TAKEAWAYS TO REMEMBER

**Focus on the economy of you.** Before you worry about what the media and financial reports are saying, you need to focus on what's happening in your personal and family financial situation so you can make the right plans to get ahead. This is how you should always make your financial decisions. Do you have an emergency fund in place? Do you have debt you need to pay off? What are your financial goals? What are your long-term investment objectives? What is your risk tolerance? Don't let panic from things outside of your control set in; instead, focus on creating a plan that you can execute to get you where you want to be.

**Pay off debt and save for a rainy day.** Create a plan to pay off any recurring high-interest debt you might have and build up your emergency fund before you ramp up your investing. The interest rates on debt can sometimes be much higher than any returns you would make investing. Also, because investing should always be for the long term, you want to make sure you have a solid emergency fund in place to carry you through in the event of unplanned life occurrences. This way, you don't have to tap into investments when those life events come up.

**Plan for the short term.** Put any money you need in the short term (less than five years) in more stable short-term financial vehicles like certificates of deposit and savings accounts. This money should not be invested in the stock market. The last thing you want is to need the money for a short-term goal when the market is going through a decline.

**Determine your risk tolerance.** When you invest your money, you assume the risk of losing part (or even all) of your investment, and that's why it's important to determine your risk tolerance to make sure your tolerance level is in line with your investment objectives. This way, you don't lose sleep every time there is a short-term market dip. The longer you keep your money invested, the longer it has to grow and the longer it has to recover in the event of a market downturn like a recession.

**Understand your investment fees.** Fees can add up over the lifetime of your investment if care is not taken. I'm talking tens or even hundreds of thousands of dollars depending on how much you have invested over time. So, it's important to understand the different fees associated with your investments and to shop around to ensure you're getting the best deal. As discussed earlier, some fee types include brokerage commissions for buying and selling your investments, annual maintenance fees typically based on a percentage of your portfolio, and management fees for any investment advisors managing your portfolio.

**Invest in funds instead of individual stocks.** Unless you have several hours each day to monitor your stocks or have a strong understanding of the stock market, it's a better idea to invest in funds like index funds or ETFs. Investing in funds can help you create a well-diversified portfolio, as they typically include a wide variety of stocks or bonds. Don't forget to do your research to understand the composition, objectives, and fees associated with the funds you are interested in investing in.

**Rebalance your portfolio.** To make sure you are staying on top of your investment objectives and timeline, set annual or more frequent reminders to review your portfolio in order to determine if it needs to be rebalanced. As the market changes and fluctuates, you'll want to ensure that your investments are balanced according to your long-term strategy.

**Diversify your portfolio.** It's important to have a well-diversified investment portfolio to spread out the potential risk of investing and to hedge your portfolio as well as possible from severe losses. That means your investments should not all be tied up in one stock, asset class, or industry. You want to make sure your investments are spread across multiple industries and areas so that if one industry or area experiences a decline, it doesn't completely sink your entire portfolio.

**Don't stop educating yourself.** Do not, under any circumstances, invest your money in any stocks or funds or business ideas that you do not understand. Do your research, learn as much as you can, and understand where you are putting your money before you make any investing decisions. Continue to expand your investing knowledge as you become a more experienced investor. Books, podcasts, video content, courses—there are so many ways to learn. The more you know, the less you fear.

**Talk about investing.** Share what you learn and engage in conversations about investing with likeminded friends, family members, and colleagues. Make investing and wealth building one of the recurring conversations you have with your partner. If you have children, as you learn about finances and investing, share the knowledge with them and involve them on your journey.

**Focus on long-term investing to build lasting wealth.** When you give your money time to work for you in the stock market, it can take advantage of the power of compounding and investment value growth. The stock market's average rate of return over the long term has been ~8% regardless of the market dips, but the key here is "long-term."

Remember, investing is how you build real wealth and is an essential way for you to achieve your financial objectives. It's not something to be afraid of, and as long as you stick with it for the long term, do your research, and stay on top of your investments, you'll be just fine. Continue to educate yourself on finances as much as possible and seek professional guidance as needed. You've got this, clever girl!

# Index

1-fund portfolio, 139–140
2-fund portfolio, 140
3-fund portfolio
  benefits, 137–138
  components, 136, 138
  investing strategy, 136–139
  investment allocation, 138
  structuring, examples, 139
3-Jar system, usage, 171
4-fund portfolio, 140–141
4% rule/withdrawal rate, 128–129
5-fund portfolio, 141
10/40/50 rule, usage, 50
*10 Prosperity Secrets for the Young and Fly* (Byrd), 170
52-week high/low, 91
80/20 investment approach, 139
100 minus your age rule, 138, 151
401(k) plan, 15, 18, 106, 114–115
  avoidance, 16
  contribution match, 170
  contributions, 130–131
  fees, 90
  investment, 49, 99, 113–114
  loan, payment, 126
  one-participant 401(k) plan, 118–119
  solo 401(k) plan, 118–119
403(b) plan, 105, 106, 115
  fees, 90
457(b) plan, 115
459(b) plan, fees, 90

Advisor risk, absence, 137
After-tax income, investment, 131
Aggressive investor, 62–63
Alexander, Faneisha (interview), 129–132
American Stock Exchange (AMEX), 22
Annual report filings (access), SEC website (usage), 87
Appreciation, 8

Assertive investor, 62–63
Asset allocation
  change, gains/losses (impact), 150
  leverage, 63

Bankruptcy, types, 154
Bank, saving (importance), 13
Bear markets
  impact, 28
  occurrence, timing, 28
Beta, 92
Betterment (robo-advisor), account (opening), 49
Bitcoin, money (losses), 31
Bogleheads, 136
*Bogleheads' Guide to the Three-Fund Portfolio, The* (Larimore), 139
Bogle, Jack, 76–77, 136
Bonds
  definition, 21
  investing, 70
  issuer. *See* Borrower.
  purchase, question, 73–74
  rating
    chart, 72
    definition, 72
  risk assessment, 72
  terms, understanding, 70–73
  types, 71–72
Borrower (bond issuer), definition, 70
Brokerage
  account fees, 89
  fees, 74
Brokerage firms
  examples, 100
  investment account, opening, 99
  selection/usage, 92, 101
  usage, 99–101
Brokers, types, 100–101
Buffett, Warren, 77, 131, 173
Bull markets
  impact, 28
  occurrence, timing, 28

Business venture, investment, 7
Byrd, Regina (interview), 170–173

Canada
    government bonds, 73
    index funds, types, 81
    retirement accounts, 120–121
    S&P/TSX indices, 25
    Toronto Stock Exchange (TSX),
        23
Canadian Registered Retirement
        Savings Plan (RRSP), 120
Capital gains, 40
    tax, 159–160
Cash supply, increase (impact), 37
Certificates of deposit, 177
Chapter 9 bankruptcy, 154
Chapter 11 bankruptcy, 154
Charity, giving, 50
Chartered SRI Counselor (CSRIC)
        (Coombs), 30
Children, investing (teaching), 171
CIBC Canadian Index, 81
*Clever Girl Finance* (Sokunbi), 93, 167
Coca-Cola, historical perfor-
        mance, 87, 88f
Common stock, 67
Companies
    bankruptcy, declaration, 154
    cash flow, 91
    financial situation/plans, under-
        standing, 86–87
    historical performance, 87
    investing decisions, 86
    IRA, cashing out, 125
    objectives/performance
        projections, 88
    profits, reporting, 87
    short-term growth/long-term
        growth potential, 67
    types, 69–70
Compounding, 17, 37, 39
    effects, loss, 125
    process, 40–44
    scenarios, usage, 48
Compound interest
    calculator, usage, 48
    debt, relationship, 46–47
Conservative investor, 62
Consumer Price Index (CPI), 36
Contributions, employer match, 16

Coombs, Jennifer N. (interview),
        30–31, 102, 153
Corporate bonds, 72
Costs, increase (impact), 37
CPI. *See* Consumer Price Index
Credit card debt, example, 47

Day trading, 104
Debt
    absence, achievement, 49
    advice, 50
    expense, increase, 47
    high-interest debt, payment
        (investment factor), 55–56
    impact, 46–47
    leverage, avoidance, 55
    payment, 92–93, 177
        commitment, 96
    payoff process, focus
        (adjustment), 130
    repayment plan/strategy, 64, 130
    snowball method, usage, 130
Demand, increase (impact), 37
Derivatives. *See* Swaps
Disability insurance, protections, 56
Discount brokers, 100
Diversification
    increase, 136, 140
    index fund diversification, 78
    leverage, 63
    opportunity, 8
    portfolio diversification, 179
Dividends, 8, 17
    earning, 21
    reinvestment/compounding, 40
    yield, 91
Dollar, value
    decline, 38
    determination, Rule of 72 (usage), 46
Dow Jones Industrial Average
        (DJIA), 24

Early retirement, examples, 112–114
Earnings
    company payments, 40
    diversification, opportunity, 8
    maximization, 63
Earnings per share (EPS), 91
Economy
    bear/bull markets, impact, 29
    impact, process, 26–29

inflation, impact, 26–27
interest rates, changes (impact), 27
market bubbles, impact, 29
stock market, relationship, 26
Emergency savings, availability
    (investment factor), 55
Emotions, usage (mistake), 168
Employer
    contribution match, usage, 123
    employer-provided 401(k),
        impact, 131
    employer-sponsored retirement
        plan, 15, 16
    job exit, actions, 122–123
    plan, money (rollover), 122–123
    retirement accounts, contri-
        butions, 116
    retirement plan, 117–118
        contribution matching, 56
Environmental, social, and govern-
    ance (ESG) factors, consid-
    eration, 31
EPS. *See* Earnings per share
Exchange-traded funds (ETFs),
    74, 75, 106
    expense ratios, 90, 137
    setup, 77
    usage, 136, 141
Expense ratios, 90

Face value, definition, 71
Federal income taxes, calculation/
    obligation, 162
Fees
    types, 89–90
    understanding. *See* Investments.
Females and Finances, 167
FICA taxes, payment, 162
Fidelity Real Estate Index Fund
    (FSRNX), 80, 141, 143
Fidelity S&P 500 Index Fund (FXAIX),
    80, 140, 142
Fidelity US Bonds Index Fund
    (FSITX), 140, 142
Fidelity ZERO International Index
    Fund (FZILX), 142
Fidelity Zero Total Market Index Fund
    (FZROX), 80, 140, 142
Finances, game-change, 15–18
Financial advice, women (treat-
    ment), 11–12

Financial advisor
    interaction, 10, 99, 102–103
    questions, 103
    research, 102–103
Financial crisis/collapse (2008),
    impact, 94, 113
Financial goals, 9
    change, 150
    investment objectives, rela-
        tionship, 58
Financial objectives, change, 150
Financial obligations, meeting
    (investment factor), 55
Financial outcomes, achievement,
    135
Financial responsibility, teaching,
    171
Financial wellness, investing
    (impact), 170–171
Food, expense, 49
frugalchiclife.com, 149
Full-service brokers, 100
Fundamentals, worsening, 154
Funds. *See* Investment
    investment, 178
    stop-loss limit, 153
    types, 142–143
Futures, 21

Gambling, investing (comparison),
    3–4, 60–61
Gender wage gap, 11
    impact (overcoming), investing
        (usage), 14
Generational wealth, building (goals/
    strategy), 171, 172
Girl Talk with Fo (Alexander), 129
gradmoney.org, 102, 153
Growth
    achievement, 149 150
    strategic investing, 13–14

Hatcher, Nicole, 149
Health insurance, usage, 56
Hickerson, Sheryl, 167–168
High-interest debt, payment (invest-
    ment factor), 55–56

Income, earning (investment
    factor), 54
Income tax, 159–160

Index funds, 74–75
  benefits, 77–79
  diversification, 78
  expenses, 88–90
    ratios, 90, 137
    reduction, 77–78
  fees, 88–90
  financial situation/plans, under-
      standing, 86–87
  historical performance, 87
  historical returns, 78
  history, 76–77
  manager risk, absence, 137
  objectives/performance pro-
      jections, 88
  passive management, 77–78
  setup, 77
  types, 79–81
  usage, 136, 144
    investment strategy creation, 17
Indices (indexes). *See* Stock indices
Individual Retirement Account (IRA)
  Canadian retirement accounts,
      comparison, 120–121
  money, rollover, 17
  Roth IRA, 117
  Simplified Employee Pension (SEP/
      SEP IRA), 117–118
  traditional IRA, 116–117
Inflation, 36–37
  beating, 13, 39
  causes, 37
  impact, 26–27
  measurement/definition, 36
  protection, 71
  rate, factoring, 44
  Rule of 72, relationship, 46
  US inflation, 38–39
Insurance coverage, investment
    factor, 56
Interest
  compounding, impact,
      40–44, 55–56
  definition, 71
  payments, 8
    determination, Rule of 72
      (usage), 46
Interest rates
  changes, impact, 27
  increase, 71
International bond funds, 143

International stock funds, 142
Investing
  3-fund portfolio investing
      strategy, 136–139
  100 minus your age rule, 138, 151
  action, 5
  advice, 50, 106–107, 132
  approach, 3–4, 131
    considerations, 30
    simplification, 144
  automation, preparation, 10
  complexities, navigation, 30
  concepts, understanding, 35–36
  continuation, examples, 40–44
  contributions, women/men
      (contrast), 12
  discussion, 179
  early investing, usage, 95
  education, 9–11
  emotion, usage (mistake), 168
  fears, overcoming, 94, 106
  gambling, comparison, 3–4, 60–61
  goals, advice, 145
  impact, 170–171
  importance, 7–9, 50
  language acquisition,
      comparison, 4
  mindset, importance, 172–173
  mistakes
    avoidance, 168–170
    recovery, 94
  perspective, 3
    notebook/spreadsheet, usage, 5
  plans, acceleration, 49
  power, leverage, 14
  practice, simulation accounts
      (usage), 103–104
  preparation, 53
    factors, 54–58
  question, 61
  research, investment factor,
      56–57
  self-directed investing, 94
  story, examples, 15–18, 105–106
  strategies
    alternatives, 139–143
    example, 106
  stress, avoidance, 62
  terms/definitions, 90–92
  time, determination, 61
  trading, contrast, 104–105

waiting, avoidance, 168
women, investing (importance), 11–15
Investment objectives, 64
  clarity, 61
  costs, calculation, 58–59
  setting, 58–59
Investment portfolio
  building, process/factors, 93, 130–131
  quarterly review, 155
  value maintenance/growth, 64
Investment risk
  mitigation, 63–64
  reduction/minimization, 151, 152
  understanding, 86
Investments. *See* Retirement investments
  approach, 49
  calculator, usage, 58
  caution, 30–31
  considerations, 90
  decisions, ESG factors (consideration), 31
  diversification
    opportunity, 8
    plan, investment factor, 57–58
  doubling, determination, 45
  expenses/fees, 88–90
  fees, understanding, 178
  fundamentals, worsening, 154
  funds, types, 74–76
  gains, 17
  gap, 11–15
  goals, example, 95
  investment-grade bond, stability, 73
  investor consideration, 31
  long-term buy-and-hold investment strategy, usage, 104–105
  long-term goals, example, 106
  losses, reduction, 153–155
  management, trust (problem), 169
  money, losses, 35
  mutual fund decisions, 74
  overnight returns, expectations (mistake), 169
  rate of return, 40
  research, 85
    process, 86–90

sale, losses, 53
strategy, 135–136
  creation, 17
  example, 94–95
timeframe
  clarity, 59
  defining, 58
value, loss (possibility), 59
worth, example, 40–41
Investopedia, stock market game, 103
Investors
  considerations, 31
  Rule of 72, importance, 46
  types, 62–63

Johnson Chandler, Kalyn, 112, 114
Journey to Launch, 143

Large-cap companies, 69
Larimore, Taylor, 139
Leadership track records, 90
Long-term buy-and-hold investment strategy, usage, 104–105
Long-term financial goals, 50
  money, usage, 11
Long-term investing
  focus, 179–180
  goals, defining/achievement, 144
Long-term wealth, building, 21
Losing investment, divestment, 153–155

Managed mutual funds, 74
Management/advisory fees, 90
Market. *See* Bear markets; Bull markets
  bubbles, impact, 29
  capitalization (market cap)
    leverage, example, 69
    stocks, relationship, 68–70
  correction, 92
  timing, mistake, 169
Market Watch, virtual stock exchange, 103
Maturity date, definition, 71
Media mentions, importance, 90
Mergers arbitrage, examination, 94–95
Midcap companies, 69–70
Millennium Asset Management Corp, 92

Money
  accumulation, payroll deductions
    (impact), 16
  earning, approaches, 7
  growth, examples, 41, 43
  investment location, example, 144
  losses, 17
  management, outsourcing
    decision, 10
  rollover, 122–123
  short-term planning, 177
  value (reduction), inflation
    (impact), 38
Money School, 171
Mothers, personal finances/generational
    wealth (improvement), 172
Municipal bonds, 72
Mutual funds, 74, 75, 106
  managed mutual funds, 74
  transaction fees, 90

National Association of Securities
    Dealers Automated Quotation
    System (NASDAQ), 22–23
  NASDAQ Composite, 24
New York Stock Exchange
    (NYSE), 22, 69
Non-retirement account, 119, 144
  investment focus, 17
  mistakes, 16–17
Non-taxable retirement account,
    withdrawal (income tax), 125

Omole, Adeola (interview), 92–96
One-participant 401(k) plan, 118–119
Online-only brokers. See Robo-advisors
Options, 21
  market, investing, 95

Partial retirement, 111
Patience, importance, 149, 153
Payroll deductions, impact, 16
Personal economy, focus, 177
Personal investment strategy, 31
Portfolio. See Investment portfolio
  1-fund portfolio, 139–140
  2-fund portfolio, 140
  3-fund portfolio investing
    strategy, 136–139
  4-fund portfolio, 140–141
  5-fund portfolio, 141

construction, 14
  diversification, 179
  economy, impact (process), 26–29
  income, earning, 7
  rebalancing, 149, 155, 178–179
    frequency, 151–152
    timing, 150–151
  risk, minimization, 61
  value, examples, 41–44
Preferred stock, 67, 68
Pre-tax retirement account, maximi-
    zation, 143
Price/book ratio, 91
Price-to-earnings ratio (P/E ratio), 91
Prosper with Regina LLC, 170

Rate of return (RoR)
  definition, 40
  Rule of 72, relationship, 45
  stock market rate of return, 57
RBC Canadian Index Fund A, 81
Real Estate Investment Trusts (REITs),
    76, 79, 80, 106, 141
  index funds, 143
  research, 170–171
Rebalancing, process, 149–150
Recession (2008), 105
Recession, impact, 61
Rent, expense, 49
Retirement, 111
  account, rollover, 122
  contribution, maximization, 124
  enjoyment, 112
  goal, approach, 150–151
  investing, 128–129
  monthly amount, determina-
    tion, 126–127
  non-retirement account,
    16–17, 119
  non-taxable retirement account,
    withdrawal (income tax), 125
  plan investments, non-retirement
    investment accounts/savings
    (combination), 17–18
  tax obligation, 162
  withdrawal rate, 128–129
Retirement investments
  accounts, types, 114–122
  diversification, 124
  maximization, advice, 123–126
  rollover, 124

Retirement savings
    achievement, example, 143
    borrowing/withdrawing,
        avoidance, 124–125
    contribution, 123
    growth, 131
    plan, 129
    projection, 127
Returns, earning, 13, 125
Risk. *See* Investment risk
    assumption, 68
    avoidance, 60
    mitigation, 60–64, 149–150
    understanding, 59–60
Risk tolerance, 151
    description, 131
    determination, 62–64, 178
    understanding, 53
Robo-advisors (online-only brokers),
        usage, 49, 99–101, 152
Rollover, 122
    IRA rollover, 17
Roth 401(k), 116
Roth IRA, 117, 144
RRSP. *See* Canadian Registered
        Retirement Savings Plan
Rule of 72, 44–46
    capabilities, 46
    debt, relationship, 46–47
    definition, 45

Sales loads, 90
Savings. *See* Retirement savings
    account, usage, 93
    advice, 50, 177
    amount, determination, 126–127
    emergency savings, availability
        (investment factor), 55
    US savings bonds, 71
Savings accounts
    interest rate, national average, 38
    long-term success, 7
Schwab International Index
        (SWISX), 142
Schwab S&P 500 Index Fund
        (SWPPX), 81, 140, 142
Schwab Total Stock Index Market
        Fund (SWTSX),
        80–81, 140, 142
Schwab US Aggregate Bond Index
        Fund (SWAGX), 140, 142

Scotia Canadian Index, 81
Self-directed investing, 94
Self-employed retirement plan, 117–119
Series EE bonds, 71
Series I bonds, 71
Short-term gains, potential, 75
Short-term goals, money (allo-
        cation), 59
Short-term life changes, plan
        (investment factor), 56
Simplified Employee Pension (SEP/
        SEP IRA), 117–118
Simulation accounts, usage,
        103–104, 105
Small-cap companies, 70
Smart Dollar Challenge, 113
Solo 401(k) plan, 118–119
Souffrant, Jamila (interview), 143–145
Standard & Poor's 500 (S&P500)
        Index, 24, 74
    index fund tracking, example, 75
    investment, 79
    stock market return, average, 38–39
Standard & Poor's TSX (S&P/TSX)
        60, 25
    Composite Index, 25
    Venture Composite Index, 25
Stock exchange
    location, 23
    stock market, contrast, 22
    types, 22–23
Stock indices (indices/indexes), 23–26
    definition, 24
    types, 24
Stock market
    action, 29
    crash (2008), impact, 87
    defining, 21–22
    earning process, 8
    economy, relationship, 26
    indices, relationship, 23–26
    investing, 95
        preparation, 53
    investments
        approach, 85–86, 99
        gamble, 54
    long-term performance, expec-
        tations, 57
    stock exchange, contrast, 22
    US stock market, return
        average, 57

Stocks
definition, 21
investing, 67–68
investments, 178
value, increase, 150
market capitalization, relationship, 68–70
purchase, determination, 73–74
stop-loss limit, 153
types, 67–68
value, factors, 67
volatility, 92
Stop-loss limit, 153
Student loans, payment (focus), 49, 130
Supercharged Financial
Strategy, usage, 93
Swaps (derivatives), 21–22

Target-date funds (age-based
fund), 152
Taveras, Jully-Alma (interview), 105–107
Taxable investing, index funds
(usage), 144
Taxes
bracket, change (prediction), 160
calculations, examples, 162
consideration, absence (mistake), 169
IRS brackets/rates (2020), 161
losses, 160
management (ease), index funds
(impact), 78–79
obligation, minimization, 161–163
tax-deferred retirement contributions, increase (determi-
nation), 163
types, 159–160
Tax-Free Savings Account (TFSA),
120, 121–122
TD Canadian Index e-series, 81
TFSA. See Tax-Free Savings Account
Thomas, Yezmin, 113, 114
Thought process, 15
Timeframe. See Investment
Toronto Stock Exchange (TSX), 23.
See also Standard &
Poor's TSX
Trade commissions, 89
Trading
day trading, 104
investing, contrast, 104–105

Traditional IRA, 116–117
Transportation, expense, 49
Treasury bonds/notes, 71

United States
bond funds, 142
government bonds, 71–72
inflation, 38–39
savings bonds, 71
stock funds, 142
stock market, return (average), 57

Value stocks, discount, 94
Vanguard 500 Index Fund (VFIAX),
79, 140, 142
Vanguard, index fund creation, 76–77
Vanguard Real Estate Index Fund
(VGSLX), 79–80, 141, 143
Vanguard Total Bond Market Fund
(VBTLX), 136, 140, 142
Vanguard Total International Bond
Index (VTABX), 141, 143
Vanguard Total International Index
Fund (VTIAX), 142
Vanguard Total International Stock
Index Fund (VTIAX), 136
Vanguard Total Stock Market Index
Fund (VTSAX), 79,
136, 140, 142
historical performance, 87, 89f

Wage gap. See Gender wage gap
Wealth building, 47, 53
efforts, impact, 124
focus, mindset, 93–94
strategy, 26
Wilshire 5000 index, 24–25
Withdrawal rate, 128–129
Women
growth, strategic investing, 13–14
inequality issue, 11
Women, investing
advice, 95–96
demotivation, 13
importance, 11–15, 50
teaching, 171–172
Working, money (making), 7

Zero-Based Budget Coaching LLC, 48*
Zuniga, Cindy E. (interview), 48–50